BIRD

BOOK

GW00601088

Index of Birds

BOOKINABOX

Editorial Director Ian Jackson
Managing Editor Tessa Monina
Proofreader Nikky Twyman
Art Director Elaine Partington
Mac Designer Brazzle Atkins
Production Sarah Rooney and Nick Eddison

Special thanks to New Holland Publishers (UK) Ltd for their cooperation.

BIRD
BOOK

MARK GOLLEY with STEPHEN MOSS

Illustrated by David Daly

CONNECTIONS
BOOK PUBLISHING

BOOKINABOX

This edition published in Great Britain in 2006 by
Connections Book Publishing Limited
St Chad's House, 148 King's Cross Road, London WC1X 9DH
www.connections-publishing.com

Text copyright © Mark Golley and Stephen Moss 1996
Artwork copyright © New Holland Publishers (UK) Ltd 1996
This edition copyright © BOOKINABOX 2006

British Library Cataloguing-in-Publication data available on request.

ISBN 1-85906-195-8

1   3   5   7   9   10   8   6   4   2

The text in *Bird Book* is an edited version of that in *The Complete Garden Bird Book*
by Mark Golley with Stephen Moss, illustrated by David Daly, and published
in the UK by New Holland Publishers (UK) Ltd.

Phototypeset in Photina MT and Futura using QuarkXPress on Apple Macintosh
Printed in China

Contents

Introduction

Whether you live in the heart of the country or the middle of a city, birds will be attracted to your garden. Indeed, one of the greatest pleasures of owning a garden is watching the birds that visit it.

If you enjoy looking at garden birds, you're not alone. In recent years, millions of people have discovered the joys of observing bird behaviour at close range. But it's not only humans who benefit – gardens are vital for the well-being and survival of birds, too.

Britain's gardens cover more than quarter of a million hectares, making them one of our most valuable bird habitats. In spring and summer, trees, bushes and artificial nest sites provide a range of places for birds to nest and rear their young. In winter, your garden can become a vital refuge for birds, especially if you regularly supply food and water. During prolonged cold spells, this can make the difference between life and death, particularly for smaller species.

This book has two main aims: to show you how to encourage birds to visit your garden, by providing places for them to feed, drink and nest; and to enable you to identify the different species.

The first section (*Watching and Attracting Birds to Your Garden*) is full of practical advice on how to create the best habitats for birds, and provide food, water and nest sites. The second section (*Identifying the Birds*) features seventy different species, each fully illustrated, with birds shown in various different plumages and displaying different forms of behaviour. This section will help you identify the visitors to your garden, as well as informing you about their habits.

Finally, at the back of the book, you will find some useful addresses and suggestions for further reading, to help you make the most of your interest in garden birds. There's also a handy Bird Topography guide (*see page 334*), so that you can see – at a glance – what all the specific terms mean.

Watching and Attracting Birds to Your Garden

Watching Garden Birds

Look out of the window into your garden, and the chances are you'll see some birds. They may be regular visitors, such as Blue Tit, Blackbird or Robin. Or they may be unfamiliar, and tricky to identify.

So, where do you go from here? Well, the first step is to get a reliable pair of binoculars (*see pages 18–21*). Binoculars allow you to observe the birds, without being noticed, at close quarters, opening up a whole new world of interest.

It is also worth keeping a log of the birds that visit your garden. Note down the different species you see, as well as a record of the date, time of day, and how many birds are present. This will help you find out which species regularly come into your garden, and which are more casual visitors.

If you do see something unusual, jot down details of the bird, especially its size, plumage details and behaviour. Birds may stay for only a moment or two before flying off, so it is important to note down as much detail as possible. Afterwards you can use the second section of this book to identify the bird at your leisure.

Bird Behaviour

The term 'bird behaviour' refers to all the ways birds live their lives, from feeding to roosting and birdsong to courtship displays. Many types of behaviour occur on a daily basis, though some, such as migration or courtship, are seasonal.

A garden is the perfect place to study bird behaviour at close range. Whether watching tits feeding on a nut-bag or a Blackbird sunbathing, you are witnessing one aspect or another of the way birds behave.

Once you have begun to identify the different birds in your garden, your next step is to find out more about their behaviour patterns. At first this can seem rather a daunting task, but don't be put off: with a little effort you will soon begin to understand why birds behave in a particular way.

Long-tailed Tits are amongst the most sociable of birds, and are generally found in pairs or small flocks. The individuals in this group have huddled together on a branch, in order to stay as warm as possible during a cold winter's night.

▶ Birdsong has two functions: to defend a breeding territory against rival males, and to attract a mate. Like all songbirds, Robins are early risers, singing most during the hours around dawn, although they can often be heard later in the day as well.

◀ During spring, look out for birds carrying nesting material in their beaks. Spotted Flycatchers often build nests in tree hollows or cracks in walls. They use bits of grass and small twigs, and line the nest with feathers.

▼ Birds' feathers get dirty very easily, and need frequent cleaning to keep them in good condition. This House Sparrow is using a birdbath to wash the city grime from its plumage. If you have a birdbath, make sure you change the water frequently, to prevent it getting too dirty.

Binoculars

A quick glance through any of the regular monthly bird magazines will leave you reeling at the vast range of binoculars that are now available. Obviously, if you are interested in just looking at birds in your garden, then it is perhaps a little extravagant to spend large amounts for a top-of-the-range pair. There is, however, a wide variety of reasonably priced, lightweight, easy-to-use binoculars which are ideally suited to your needs.

But how do you decide which binoculars are for you? The ideal thing to do is to go to one of the many specialist shops that deal in optical equipment. Explain to staff what you are looking for, how much you are willing to pay and what you will use them for, and they will know what to suggest.

For birds in the garden, you do not need to choose a 'big' pair of binoculars. The magnification need only be around 8 x 30 – and these will give you clarity, a good, bright image, and they should be nice and light. Choose the binoculars you feel most comfortable with, the ones that feel 'right' in your hands, be they Porro prism, roof prism or a more compact design.

Porro prism The 'traditional'-looking binoculars in a style which, despite refinements, has not really changed for decades. Often, these binoculars can be heavy, bulky and a little impractical for use, especially if you are looking out of the kitchen window. The magnifications vary, from 7 x 50 upwards to 12 x 50 and beyond, but there are many Porro prism binoculars that fall into the ideal category – usually 8 x 30 – and so certainly bear these in mind.

Compact binoculars Perhaps the best option for simple enjoyment of birds in your garden is a pair of neat, very easy-to-use, very lightweight, 'put-them-in-your-pocket', compact binoculars. What they lack in magnification, often only up to 7 x 26, they make up for in the ways noted above. Some of the leading manufacturers of optics have now turned their eyes to this end of the market.

Roof prism Often at the expensive end of the scale, roof-prism binoculars tend to be favoured by birdwatchers as they are easier to hold, with regard to both shape and weight. Not all roof-prism binoculars will have the bank manager seeing red, but, as you may expect, quality is not so good at the lower end of the market.

Ideal Garden Habitats

Whenever possible, it is always worthwhile trying to bring some diversity of habitat into your garden. If you have a lawn, pure and simple, what about putting aside some space to plant some shrubs or trees, or be brave and dig out a pond! If you already have a garden with trees in it, how about trying to plant up a hedge along the outside of your garden?

Trees, hedges and shrubs are all very important habitats for garden birds. They provide natural cover, offer potential nesting places and are a tremendous food source. Of course there are hundreds of choices, but are there some that are better than others? Here, we investigate this (*see pages 25–7*).

If you have the resources, a pond will add another dimension to your garden and the birdlife in it. Ponds will quickly attract insects, on which birds will thrive, and of course you have a ready-made birdbath and drinking pool. Remember that water is as vital to birds as worms, seeds, grain or nuts are, and it should never be forgotten.

And if you don't have any trees, hedges or ponds in your garden, don't panic. A lawn will have enough food in it to keep the local Blackbird happy at the very least, and even in the most urban setting birds can still be enticed into your garden to feed.

The best way to attract birds to your garden is to provide as good a selection of plants as possible. Plants are valuable for several reasons. They provide shelter and cover, enabling birds to roost at night, and their thick foliage also enables nesting birds to protect their eggs and chicks against various predators.

Whatever the season, garden plants provide a ready

source of food, including seeds, berries, fruit and nectar. One way to help birds survive the winter months is to plant a variety of berry-bearing shrubs in your garden (*see opposite*).

Plants also play an important role by attracting insects, another vital source of food, especially for smaller birds such as tits and warblers. You should choose plants suitable for insects, such as Buddleia, often known as the butterfly bush because its flowers are so attractive to butterflies.

You can also attract birds to your garden by creating a pond. Even a small garden pond provides a place for birds to drink and bathe, as well as attracting a variety of insects. A pond is surprisingly simple to make, and can be built in even the smallest of gardens.

◀ **Blackberries** come into their own in the autumn. The plump delicious fruit will be welcomed by both resident and migrant thrushes, all of which will have a field day feeding on the berries.

▶ The **Birch** catkins of early spring are popular with some of the smaller finches, Siskins and Redpolls particularly. In winter, when the tree loses its leaves, woodpeckers often become regular visitors to birch trees, finding the wood easy to penetrate for insects.

◀ The **Wild Cherry** offers juicy fruit in the autumn. Bullfinches enjoy nibbling at the flesh, before tackling the hard stone inside. The beautiful flowers attract insects for pollination, which in turn attract birds – warblers particularly.

▶ In spring and summer, a whole host of species ranging from woodpeckers to warblers can breed in **Oaks**, with vast numbers of small caterpillars providing enormous amounts of food for parent birds to take back to hungry broods.

◀ Both the **Norway Spruce** and the **Sitka Spruce** are popular with several species of bird, most notably Goldcrest, Coal Tit, Treecreeper, Nuthatch and finches.

▶ **Wild crab apples** are an invaluable source of food for thrushes in hard weather. Redwings and Fieldfares will devour the flesh and leave the pips for Chaffinches and tits.

◀ The **Hawthorn** is a 'dense' tree, offering protection for species that choose to nest inside. The haws themselves are a food source for finches and thrushes, and add colour to the garden.

Gardens are an important refuge for insects, especially if you avoid using powerful insecticides. Try to keep at least part of the garden in a 'wild' state, letting the native weeds take over. You may not be popular with your neighbours, but the insects – and the birds – will thank you for it! Bear in mind also that many of the plants that we tend to call 'weeds' are actually very attractive when in flower, and can certainly add to the visual appeal of a garden.

Birds feed on a wide variety of insects, depending mainly on the size of their bill. Occasionally greed will overcome a bird's better judgement, and it will attempt to eat an insect far too big for it to manage. Nevertheless, birds are able to swallow surprisingly big items with apparent ease.

Urban Gardens

Even if your garden is just a tiny patch of green in a city centre, it can still attract birds. Think of it as a welcome oasis, providing shelter, food and sometimes also a place to nest. Make your garden as 'bird-friendly' as possible to increase the number and variety of visitors: provide birdtables, birdbaths and nestboxes, and try to keep out unwelcome visitors such as cats and squirrels.

In early spring, birds such as House Sparrows are looking for bits and pieces with which to build their nests. In towns and cities, these may be in short supply, but you can help by providing alternative materials such as wool or hair.

Hard winter weather often drives birds to seek refuge in gardens, where a guaranteed supply of food and water can make the difference between life and death. As well as larger numbers of the regular species, your garden may play host to more unusual visitors, such as Coal Tit, woodpeckers or this Nuthatch, seen here in characteristic pose on a nutbag. If harsh weather persists, these birds may remain in the garden for some time, provided that food and water are in constant supply.

Parks and Open Spaces

Once you have begun to get to grips with the birds in your garden, you will probably want to venture further afield. A good place to start is your local park, where you can see a wider variety of species, and test your new-found identification skills.

Go during a busy summer weekend, and there won't be many birds around. But pay a visit early in the morning, before the children and dog-walkers are out and about, and you'll find a very different scene. This is when most birds are very active, feeding, singing and calling, bathing, preening and so on, and they are often relatively tame as well, so you'll find you can approach them more closely.

◄ The Hawfinch is one of our shyest birds, and is best looked for at a known breeding or wintering site. Listen out for its distinctive call, an explosive *zik*. Hawfinches are often seen singly or in small flocks near the tops of trees.

► About the size of a sparrow, the Lesser Spotted Woodpecker is our smallest woodpecker, and the hardest to see. It is best looked for in winter, when it may join a flock of tits and other small birds in search of food. In spring, listen for its soft drumming in wooded areas.

In spring, breeding birds will be singing before dawn. Bird sounds can be confusing for a beginner, so it is worth spending some time getting to know the different calls and songs, perhaps using CDs or tapes. Singing birds are frequently difficult to see because of dense foliage, but be patient, and they will eventually reveal themselves.

Larger parks and open spaces will support an even greater variety of birdlife, though you may have to search for some time before you see any of the more elusive species.

If your local park has a pond or lake, this will attract ducks and other waterfowl, especially in autumn and winter. These birds are usually less prone to human disturbance than songbirds, and may allow very close approach, especially if you bring some bread to feed them! Most likely species are Tufted Duck, Pochard, Mallard, Shoveler, Moorhen and Coot, and the ubiquitous Canada Goose.

Feeding Birds

Attracting birds into your garden, however big or small, is something that will bring you endless hours of enjoyment and pleasure. Roving flocks of birds pass through gardens with some regularity, but how do you keep them in your garden for that little bit longer? And what can you do to ensure that the birds will keep coming back into your garden?

A guaranteed way of enticing birds into your garden over and over again is simply to feed them. As 'word goes around' that food is available in your garden, more and more birds will pay a visit and you should soon see a marked increase in activity. But what should you feed them, and when? And are there particular foods that should be put out in winter and not in summer, or vice versa?

This section covers all those queries and quandaries, giving you the best advice with regard to 'safe' foods and, it is hoped, some new ideas on keeping the birds in your garden fed and watered. From birdtables to seed hoppers, birdbaths to 'tit bells' and scrap baskets, there are various successful ways to feed your garden visitors.

Robins are undoubtedly one of the most popular visitors to any garden. Highly adaptable, they will return to the garden for food whatever the time of year. If space is limited, place food into a terracotta bowl, which has the advantage of being frostproof. Time and time again birds will repay your patience by becoming more trusting and approachable.

A birdtable is one of the most traditional and familiar methods of attracting birds into your garden. Birdtables come in all sorts of shapes and sizes – with or without sides, with or without perches, sometimes with a roof (often thatched), and some even have a nestbox included! They can attract many different species – here we have Great Tit, House Sparrow and Chaffinch – and they can all gain plenty of nourishment from foodstuffs left out for them. They will feed on different items, but do try to adapt to them all.

▶ In winter months you can gain so much pleasure from gazing out of the kitchen window (never mind the washing-up!) watching birds squabble and feed on a nutbag. Here we see a Siskin encountering a Great Tit and a Blue Tit, all of them vying for the choicest peanuts.

▼ Water is as vital to a bird's survival as a good store of food, particularly in winter. A birdbath (anything from a dustbin lid to a purpose-built birdbath) gives birds a place to bathe and keep their feathers in good working order, and provides an essential source of drinking water. This Song Thrush is making full use of the bath (kept ice-free in winter by a 'night light' placed underneath).

◄ Some species are not too fussy about their diet, and will eat more or less whatever you give them. These Starlings are feeding on kitchen scraps, hung up in a basket to avoid attracting rats or mice.

► Seeds are the staple diet of finches such as Greenfinch and Goldfinch. Their different-shaped bills are specially adapted to eat particular seeds, so make sure that you provide a variety of shapes and sizes – and in reasonable quantity if you wish the birds to return!

◄ One of the best ways to observe birds is by using a window feeder. Birds like this Robin and Blue Tit will soon get used to it, allowing you to watch them in dramatic close-up from the comfort of your living room!

► A tit bell crammed with fat or suet is a good way to provide a high-energy food for these tiny birds, which may need to eat as much as a quarter or even more of their body weight every day in order to survive cold weather. In harsh winters, many tits would perish without such provisions.

▶ A hollow stick pierced with small holes and filled with suet, available from many good bird-food suppliers, may attract scarcer species such as Nuthatch and Great Spotted Woodpecker to your garden, particularly in the winter months and especially if you live not too far from a wood, even a small one.

▼ Mealworms, available from pet stores and fishing supply stores, are an ideal high-energy winter food for many species of bird, including tits, thrushes and this hungry Blackbird.

Nest Sites

One of the best ways of attracting birds to your garden is by providing sites where they can raise their young. Trees, shrubs, holes in the wall, even old drainpipes, can all be suitable places to build a nest. Even a small garden can support as many as half a dozen nests, while a larger garden, with a variety of habitats, is a valuable refuge for breeding birds.

Keen gardeners can encourage birds to nest by planting a variety of suitable shrubs and trees. Native plants such as Elder and Hawthorn are usually best, although fast-growing evergreens such as cypresses can provide cover, too.

Birds don't only build their nests in natural sites; they will also take readily to man-made nestboxes. These come in all shapes and sizes, each designed to attract a particular species while at the same time preventing others from using the box.

It is usually best to put a nestbox up during the winter, so that the birds get used to it before the breeding season begins. The best site is on a tree, wall or garden fence, between two and five metres above the ground. Nestboxes should generally face between northeast and southeast, thus avoiding the midday sun and the wettest winds. Try to place the box out of the reach of potential predators and inquisitive humans!

The RSPB provides fact sheets containing information on the several different kinds of nestboxes, with details on how to build your own. It also sells ready-made boxes by mail order, if DIY isn't your speciality! (*See page 332.*)

▶ The most widely used nestboxes have a small opening, around 25–32 mm diameter, depending on which species you want to attract. Great Tits prefer around 28 mm. They produce one or two broods, with five to eleven eggs, which the adults incubate for around a fortnight. The young fledge three weeks later.

◀ An open-fronted nestbox is suitable for species such as Robin, Wren and Spotted Flycatcher. Wrens usually lay two clutches of between five and eight eggs, although the male often has to build several nests before one is selected by his choosy mate!

◄ A decline in the number of fallen and rotten trees has drastically reduced the availability of nest sites for larger birds such as the Tawny Owl. Help redress the balance by providing specially designed owl boxes, which are fixed to the underside of branches or placed in a tree fork. These are best placed in an area where owls are known to be resident.

► This specialized nestbox, made to resemble a natural crevice in a tree trunk, is designed to attract the Treecreeper. In woodlands, a typical natural site would be behind a loose piece of bark or in ivy. This tiny, mouse-like bird is sometimes seen in rural gardens, climbing up tree-trunks in search of its insect food.

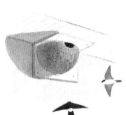

◄ House Martins are one of our most familiar summer visitors. As their name suggests, they usually build their nests under the eaves of houses, using pellets of wet mud. You can encourage them to breed by putting up artificial nests, though your neighbours may complain, as the young are very noisy!

► The Spotted Flycatcher is one of our daintiest and most interesting summer visitors, living up to its name by making acrobatic chases after its insect prey. It nests in a variety of sites, but is often attracted to hanging baskets, as well as ledges and specially designed nestboxes.

Garden Hazards

Gardens may be a welcome haven for their owners, but for birds there are few more hazardous places. The greatest villain of the piece is the domestic cat, responsible for millions of bird deaths every year. Unfortunately, the majority of cats' victims are adult birds, whose death often results in nesting failure.

Some of the major predators are other birds, attracted to gardens by the large concentration of smaller birds there. To a bird of prey like the Sparrowhawk, a birdtable looks like a free lunch.

You can take steps to reduce the carnage in your own garden by making sure that food is placed on sturdy birdtables, out of the reach of most predators.

▶ Perhaps the most notorious garden predator is the Magpie. However, they are not quite the villains they are sometimes painted as. Unlike cats, they generally prey on eggs and chicks, so, even if a brood is destroyed, the adult birds have a chance to raise a second one.

▼ Cats have a very damaging effect on the populations of many garden birds, especially during the breeding season. One way to thwart a cat's attempts is to tie a bell around its neck. This generally warns the birds of the cat's approach, and should significantly reduce the death toll.

▶ One of the most spectacular and memorable sights of garden birdwatching is a Sparrowhawk in pursuit of its prey. The hawk's short, blunt wings and long tail enable it to approach fast and unseen, at a low angle. This unsuspecting Chaffinch may never have known what hit it.

◀ There is nothing a squirrel likes quite so much as a meal of eggs or young birds. The best way to make your nestbox squirrel-proof is by fixing a sturdy metal plate over the area around the hole. This should foil all but the most determined intruder.

Identifying
the Birds

Grey Heron

90–100 cm (36–40 in)

Appearance Tall, slender and elegant, with a heavy, dagger-like bill, long legs, and grey, black and white plumage, the adult Grey Heron is a masterful-looking bird, and an impressive sight.

Behaviour Grey Herons can be found along almost all waterways, from lakes, rivers, marshes and estuaries to garden ponds, where – with their fish diet – they may not be the most welcome of visitors! Communal nesters, they often favour woodland trees as a breeding site, though also breed in reedbeds and, occasionally, on cliffs.

Call A loud, hard *frank* or *krank*, invariably called when in flight.

▶ Slim black head plumes, visible in the breeding season, extend down from the distinctive badger stripes on the crown. A black 'shoulder' and pale silvery plumes define the wing.

▲ Stockier and darker than adults, juveniles lack plumes and shoulder patch. The grey head has only a white throat for contrast. Note the olive legs.

▶ The black flank line and white belly are clearly visible during flight, the neck held hunched with long legs trailing.

▼ The nest-building and display rituals start in late January and, when presented with a suitable stick or twig, much bill-snapping and calling breaks out.

▼ The black flecks that run from throat to belly are displayed as the bird surveys its territory, shaggy breast plumes (on breeding birds) flapping in the breeze.

▲ Spot the Heron: when sleeping, they can be easy to overlook. Seemingly oblivious to disturbance, they can stay hunched up for long periods of time.

Mallard

55–62 cm (21$\frac{1}{2}$–24$\frac{1}{2}$ in)

Appearance Hefty, large-headed and long-billed, pure Mallards are easily identifiable from other dabbling ducks – even the brown female, due to its size.

Behaviour Found in any watery location, from secluded streams to boating lakes, Mallards are often very tame and will show no fear in approaching people. They are prone to interbreed with 'farmyard' ducks, so can produce all manner of peculiar-looking offspring.

Call The female is responsible for the familiar *quack quack*, whereas the male gives a low nasal whistle.

▼ The variegated brown and black pattern of the female makes them appear rather nondescript, the dark eye stripe perhaps the most distinguishing feature.

▲ The male's bottle-green head contrasts with the bright yellow bill, and is separated from the rusty-brown breast by a distinctive white neck ring.

▶ From above, the male in flight reveals a purple speculum (a contrasting patch seen on the secondaries) with two white wing bars, black rump 'wedge' and white tail. The female's speculum is darker.

◀ Familiar view: Mallards upending in search of food. The male is recognizable by his black and white rear end, while the female exhibits a white tail edge and blackish spots on the undertail.

In summer, a male
in eclipse plumage can
change appearance quite
markedly. The familiar guise
(*right*) transforms into a pale brown
head, black crown and eye stripe, dull
bill, and blackish-grey upperparts with
a black-scalloped breast (*below*).

Sparrowhawk

28–38 cm (11–15 in)

Appearance Plumage differs markedly in male and female, but both share broad, blunt, shortish wings, a 'small-headed' look and long square-ended tail, and are distinguished from other birds of prey by their dashing flight.

Behaviour Typically a bird of open countryside, this agile bird of prey is now an increasingly familiar visitor to both rural and urban gardens. Sparrowhawks are particularly adept at dashing through woodlands, along hedges and through gardens at great speed and, if successful, will often take their prey to a 'plucking post'. Adult pairs soar together during the breeding season.

Call A rapid, harsh *kek-kek-kek* alarm call.

◀ The male is smaller than the female, with russet cheeks, dark tail bars and wing tips, and finely barred orangey-red underparts.

▶ The underparts of the female show a white base with fine grey horizontal barring. The yellow eye is especially striking.

▲ Note the tail bars and wing shape in flight, and the size of the head and tail.

▲ Sparrowhawks fly with quick bursts of rapid wingbeats interspersed with short glides. When soaring, they look flat-winged and the tail is only occasionally fanned.

◀ The prey is usually carried to a plucking post, where the feathers are then torn from it and the flesh taken back to a mate or youngsters in a nest.

Juveniles can be recognized by browner upperparts, often with reddish-brown edges, and brownish-buff barring on the underparts. The eyes are greener than those of adults.

Buzzard

50–56 cm (19½–22 in)

Appearance Buzzards come in a variety of plumages, but are easily identified by their broad wings, large head, stout, hooked bill and shortish tail – and by their seemingly effortless flight manner, as they spiral into the sky.

Behaviour Their favourite habitat is mixed woodland adjacent to farmland, as it provides an ideal opportunity to nest and feed in close proximity, but they can also be seen in moorland and upland areas, and even drifting over gardens and town centres. They feed on small mammals, and can often be seen perched on top of telegraph poles or sitting in trees, watching for prey.

Call A cat-like *me-uw*, usually heard as it soars above the landscape.

◄ Pale extreme: pale underparts give way to brown flecking on the breast sides. The prominent white supercilia and throat contrast with the brownish ear-coverts on the pale head.

▶ The typical plumage is dark brown, except for paler ear-coverts and a whitish throat and lower-breast patch, with fine barring visible on the paler undertail.

▶ The wings are
held slightly above
body level, with the
tips upturned, in this highly
distinctive profile.

◀ Characteristic plumage features
include the brownish head, breast
and belly contrasting with the pale
undertail. Note the distinctive three-
toned wings.

▶ This pale bird shows dark
carpal patches and
wing tips, with a dark
trailing edge to the
wing and standard
dark tail band.

◄ From above, there is little obvious contrast. The forewing shows a darker leading edge, and a good view reveals a darker trailing edge to the wing as well as to the tip of the tail.

▶ Buzzards are good opportunist feeders, killing for themselves or taking full advantage of a death from natural causes.

Kestrel

33–36 cm (13–14 in)

Appearance These distinctive falcons are easily told from other birds of prey by their size, longish tail, noticeably pointed wings and hovering flight.

Behaviour Kestrels are found in any number of different habitats, from large cities to remote hillsides. They are perhaps most commonly seen on roadsides, hovering in search of food or perched on roadside wires, telegraph poles and fences. They nest in holes or on ledges, in both natural and man-made locations.

Call A shrill *kee-kee-kee*. It is often particularly noisy at nesting sites.

▶ The rufous and dark-barred colouring of the larger females makes them unmistakable. The cheeks and throat are white with a prominent black moustache. Both sexes share a large black eye with yellow eyering.

▶ The male's head, rump and tail are blue-grey, with a black tail tip, and the pinkish-white underparts show distinctive black 'teardrops' from upper breast to belly.

In flight, the differences between the sexes are clear. The grey of the male's head and tail contrasts strongly with the chestnut and black of the wings, as compared to the overall rufous tones of the female upperparts. Check the tail pattern, too – look for prominent dark bars (usually around six or seven) on the female.

◄ In 'normal' flight, Kestrels have a whip-like deep wingbeat interspersed with glides. When hovering, the tail fans out and points down for stability.

▼ Juveniles resemble the female, except for a redder-looking rump and bolder streaks on the underparts. Legs and feet may appear more orange in colour.

Red-legged Partridge

33–36 cm (13–14 in)

Appearance Rounder-looking and often more upright than the Grey Partridge, 'Redlegs' show a more striking head pattern, a plainer back and more complex under-part markings.

Behaviour Red-legged Partridges can be found in a variety of habitats – farmland, heathland, shingle beaches, dunes ... If you have a garden in any of these areas, don't be surprised if you see one of these birds wandering across your lawn!

Call A loud, rasping *chuck, chuck, chukak* can usually be heard as the Red-legged Partridge runs along.

The flanks are a striking mix of black, white, red and blue bars, while the belly and undertail are a rich orange. Note the red bill, eyering and legs.

▼ The stark white eye stripe and throat patch contrast markedly with the grey-brown head and bold black spotted 'necklace'.

◄ The whirring wings are always a giveaway! Red-legged Partridges fly fast and low on bowed-looking wings (although they run more than they fly). The orange on the tail is especially striking in flight.

▶ From behind, the strong black and white head markings and flank bars are easy to see, and make the Red-legged Partridge utterly distinctive.

◀ The juvenile's face pattern is very faint, the 'necklace' is replaced by sparse grey mottling, and the flanks are barred whitish and brown.

Pheasant

52–90 cm (20¹/₂–35¹/₂ in)

Appearance The colourful male, with its distinctive red eye patch, is unmistakable, but both sexes can be identified by their long pointed tails and short, rounded narrow wings.

Behaviour Pheasants are found in woodland, farmland, marshes and even reedbeds, and are often seen – particularly in the early morning or late evening – wandering serenely across gardens in more rural areas. They roost in trees at night, often in small flocks.

Call A distinctive, rapid-fire *kutuk, kutuk, kutuk* alarm, usually heard when flushed from cover.

▶ Females vary, although basic plumage patterns are similar whatever the colour. They are smaller and shorter-tailed than males.

▲ Males are also variable; most common are those with a distinctive white neck collar and glossy greenish-black head.

▶ When emerging from cover, Pheasants make a great deal of noise, crashing from the undergrowth while calling their distinctive cry. Their flight pattern is short and low to the ground, with rapid flaps and long glides.

▼ Note the widely spaced bars on the uppertail, shown in both male and female Pheasants.

From this angle, the 'ear tufts' and trademark red facial patches of the male are clearly visible. Although this particular male lacks the white neck collar, the rich copper-toned plumage is still to be admired.

Moorhen

31–35 cm (12–14 in)

Appearance These distinctive waterbirds have short wings, a bulky body, long legs and large feet, with a cherry-red frontal shield and bill (except for the yellow tip). The white flank line and gleaming white undertail are other features which make them easy to distinguish from Coots.

Behaviour Moorhens are commonly encountered on ornamental lakes, village ponds, rivers and garden streams. They are territorial birds, and fights are commonplace, whatever the season. Conflicts can last many minutes, and injuries – even fatalities – are not unknown.

Song Explosive, gurgling *kurr-uck*, *kek* and *kikik* sounds litter the air as the birds vent their anger.

▶ Bird fight: bodies tilt backwards into the water, wings flop, the feet become jousting weapons … and the noise is deafening!

◀ On land, the long legs and large feet make the Moorhen look rather ungainly, even timid. Look for a small red 'thigh' patch, often visible just above the knee.

▶ Awkward spectacle: the Moorhen's short wings and bulky body make flight difficult, and they appear very weak on the wing, long legs trailing behind.

◀ Adult Moorhens are good parents, and can be seen throughout the breeding season gently passing food to their bald-headed fluffy black chicks at the edge of ponds, rivers and reedbeds.

▼ The Moorhen moves with jerky actions and a constantly flicking tail, often dwelling to pick at the water surface, feeding on weeds, insects or seeds.

▼ Juveniles display none of the adults' greyish-black and deep brown colouring, instead showing a dirty-white chin and throat, and a greyish-brown wash on the face.

Black-headed Gull

35–38 cm (14–15 in)

Appearance These slim-looking birds have a domed head, slender bill and clearly pointed wings, with distinct summer and winter plumages for both the adults and immatures.

Behaviour Although still thought of by some as just seaside nesters, Black-headed Gulls breed in almost any wetland habitat, from inland sites such as gravel pits to coastal marshes. In the winter, they can be encountered anywhere – even stealing food from birdtables!

Call A harsh *kwarr* or *kwuririp*. The noise can be particularly deafening on breeding grounds.

▶ A first-summer bird resembles a 'mix' of adult and immature plumage, moulting out of its first-winter plumage between February and April.

◀ An adult summer bird attains its plumage in February or March. The hood is chocolate-brown, and there is a partial thin white eyering. Bill, legs and feet are dark red.

▶ A first-winter 'Blackhead': note the brown on the wings, and black tail band. Black-headed Gulls fly with a buoyant, jaunty action with fast wingbeats, and are also adept at gliding, soaring and hawking for insects.

◀ All plumages share a distinctive wing pattern: a strong white leading edge contrasting with the black trailing edge to the outer wing feathers.

▼ First-winter birds resemble adult winter ones except for more mottling on the head, and brown on the coverts, secondaries and tertials. The legs are a muddy orange.

▶ The adult winter bird shows identical plumage to the summer adult, except for the head pattern. The legs becomes dull orangey-red.

Common Gull

38–43 cm (15–17 in)

Appearance Larger than the Black-headed Gull, adult Common Gulls have the unique combination of wholly yellow bill and legs. At rest, the wing tips project well beyond the tail, giving the body a tapered appearance.

Behaviour Found in almost any location, urban or rural, coastal or inland, they are frequently seen in the company of Black-headed Gulls, particularly in the winter months, when they search for worms and insects on newly ploughed fields. In coastal habitats, they feed on fish and other aquatic life.

Call Their repetitive shrill, high-pitched *keeeyaa* is instantly recognizable.

▼ First-winter birds show heavy streaks on
the crown and cheeks, with a grey mantle,
brown wing coverts
and tertials, and
black flight
feathers.

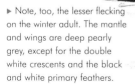

▶ Note, too, the lesser flecking
on the winter adult. The mantle
and wings are deep pearly
grey, except for the double
white crescents and the black
and white primary feathers.

▼ The striking white-marked black wing tips of the winter adult are obvious in flight. Look also for the broad white trailing edge along the wing.

▲ A bird in its second winter has more brown on the outer wing, heavy greyish blotching on the head, and duller, more olive-coloured bare parts.

▶ The young Common Gull is full of contrast, with a pale head, dark back, black, brown and grey wings, white rump and broad black tail band.

▼ In the summer, the head is gleaming white and the bill and feet are bright yellow. The eye shows a blood-red orbital ring.

Stock Dove

31–35 cm (12–14 in)

Appearance Smaller than the Woodpigeon, this neat, compact bird has a small, squarish head, plump body and beautifully subtle plumage.

Behaviour Stock Doves tend to favour woods and open farmland, but can still be found in more urban parks and gardens. They are generally a little more solitary than other doves and pigeons, and are usually seen in pairs, although they do sometimes flock.

Song The male will try to woo a female with a monotonous *coo-oh, coo-oh*.

▼ Note the dark silvery-grey head with emerald-green neck patch and salmon-pink breast patch. The pale yellow bill has a whitish knob and reddish base.

▼ The back, rump and wings are dark grey, except for black on the wing coverts and primary feathers. The tail shows a broad black tip.

◄ The soft tones of the upper- and underparts are offset by the broad black trailing edge on the upper wing and the double spots on the coverts. The black tail band is also very obvious.

► Stock Doves hold their wings straighter than Woodpigeons and have a quick, direct flight, with occasional flicks. Note the two short, dark bars on the inner wing.

They like nesting in natural tree holes, or sometimes in and around derelict buildings, and may even nest in old rabbit burrows.

Woodpigeon

39–45 cm (15½–17½ in)

Appearance This familiar, plump bird has a small head, a very full-chested look, broad wings and a longish tail. The plumage pattern is distinctive, both in flight and on the ground.

Behaviour Woodpigeons can be found in almost any sort of habitat, but favour woodlands, gardens and parkland, whether in an urban or rural situation. They are very prolific birds, producing youngsters from March through to late November if the weather is suitable, and in the autumn months huge flocks containing many hundreds of birds can be seen in agricultural areas.

Song A rhythmical, five-note sequence of *coo-coooo-coo, coo-coo*, repeated regularly.

◄ The juvenile lacks the greenish gloss on the hindneck as well as the white neck patch, and the breast is a dull buff-pink.

► The adult's head is pale blue-grey, with a distinctive green and white collar, and the purplish-pink breast fades to white on the belly area. Note the white on the forewing when the wing is closed.

▲ From above, the large white wing patches, black flight feathers and tail band are immediately apparent, in contrast to the pale underwing and pink breast visible from below.

▲ Large flocks of Woodpigeons are a common autumn sight. They take off with an almighty clatter as they leave fields or trees, and are capable of quick flight, with very deep wingbeats.

In rural areas during the early autumn, flocks of Woodpigeons are often seen out and about feeding on fields of cut corn. Farmers will go to great lengths to deter them, but these seldom have any real effect.

Collared Dove

29–32 cm (11½–12½ in)

Appearance These slim, long-tailed birds have broad wings and generally pale plumage. Sometimes confused with Turtle Doves, they are more uniformly coloured, and have a distinctive black and white half-collar.

Behaviour Originally found in Asia, the Collared Dove 'invaded' Europe in the mid 1900s, and is now found throughout Britain in large numbers. They can be seen in parks and gardens in cities, towns and villages, and often frequent farmland, or anywhere where grain is handled and spilled.

Song A distinctive *coo-coo-kut* – with the middle syllable stressed and higher-pitched and the final one short and clipped – and a drawn-out nasal *kwurr* in flight.

▼ Head and breast are a delicate shade of buffy-pink, with a pale sandy-brown mantle and grey rump, fading to buffy uppertail feathers. Some birds have extremely pale plumage, and can appear 'washed-out'.

▼ Similar in many ways, with blackish bill, black eye and white eyering, juveniles lack the familiar collar of the adult, and have greyer, more scaly-looking plumage.

◄ Collared Doves spend a lot of time perched on wires or telegraph poles. Males will 'coo' to attract a mate, while both sexes will make themselves comfortable, tucking heads in, happy to stay there all day.

► The black wing tips contrast strongly with the grey and brown inner wings. From above, the tail pattern shows white tips to all but the central feathers.

Collared Doves can often be seen drifting on their broad wings. From below, they look very pale, except for the striking broad black and white pattern on the undertail.

Feral Pigeon
31–35 cm (12–14 in)

Appearance Coming in an incredible variety of plumages, colours varying from white to black to brown to grey, in different combinations and patterns, this familiar, round-looking dove is nevertheless unmistakable.

Behaviour Feral Pigeons can be seen absolutely anywhere, but especially in towns and cities, often in large numbers. Renowned for their extreme tameness, they are perfectly happy taking food from the hand, and are also notorious for the large amounts of mess they make! They have infiltrated the Rock Dove population to drastic effect, and breed readily throughout the year.

Song A familiar *oo-roo-coo*, usually repeated several times, often with a slight increase in volume.

The blue-grey head merges into a green
sheen on the neck, and the upper breast
shows a purple gloss, in markings close to
a true Rock Dove (*below*). A familiar variant
(*right*) shows predominantly dark grey
plumage with dark and light barred wings.

A flock of Feral Pigeons gliding effortlessly over rooftops is a familiar sight in urban areas. The Feral Pigeon has a very easy, sailing flight, which is interspersed with slow and deliberate flaps and glides.

Variety show: note the familiar 'chequering' on the wing (*below right*), while at the paler end of the scale plumage ranges from pinky-buff to almost pure white.

Turtle Dove

26–29 cm (10–11½ in)

Appearance Small-headed and with a slim body, long tapering tail and variegated plumage, the Turtle Dove is a pretty and distinctive little pigeon.

Behaviour Usually shy, Turtle Doves are found in woodlands, plantations and bushy hedgerows, but will also visit large urban or rural gardens. They are summer visitors from Africa, arriving in mid April to early May, and staying until mid to late September.

Song A soft and deep purring *rrooorrr rrooorrr*, often repeated for long periods, and heard throughout late spring and early summer.

▼ The wing is rich chestnut, with bold black feather-centres, a grey forewing, and dark flight feathers.

▲ Note the delicate grey cast to the forehead, crown and nape, and several black bars with distinctive white edges on the neck.

◄ From below, the pale grey head and pink breast contrast with the dark grey and black underwings and the black and white tail.

► From above, it's a different story: grey, chestnut, black and white clash in a flurry of colour. The bold tail pattern is particularly striking.

Juvenile Turtle Doves show a buffy
head and breast, no neck bars and
more subdued brown wing markings.

Cuckoo

32–34 cm (12½–13½ in)

Appearance With its long tail and pointed wings, the Cuckoo can be confused with certain birds of prey, but note the rounded tail, small head, often held slightly upward, and thin bill. The famous song is the giveaway!

Behaviour Summer visitors from early April to mid September, Cuckoos frequent a variety of habitats, from woods to reedbeds, coastal dunes to moorland. The female lays her eggs in other garden birds' nests, and the new parent raises the huge youngster, which slowly but surely evicts the other eggs and nestlings.

Song A far-carrying *cuc-coo* called by the male, but also a stuttering *cuc-cuc-coo* and, when agitated, a gurgling *gug, gug, gug, gug*. The female has a bubbling trill.

▶ Cuckoos fly in a very direct manner, usually fairly low to the ground, but are also capable of gliding some distance.

▶ The male shows a silvery-grey head and upper breast, with dark flight feathers. Note the white notches on the tail feathers, white tail tip and barring on the underparts.

▼ Grey-phase females are identical to males except for a brownish wash on the breast and browner-looking flight feathers.

▲ The distinctive rufous-brown phase of the female is more scarce than the familiar grey. The upperparts show fine black barring from head to tail – a striking spectacle in flight.

Juvenile Cuckoos, once fledged, still take advantage of their surrogate parents' hospitality. Their plumage appears somewhat scaly, with white edges to the feathers and a white patch on the nape.

Barn Owl

33–36 cm (13–14 in)

Appearance With a slim body, long wings, long legs, white heart-shaped face and striking black eyes, this beautiful medium-sized owl appears almost ghostly, and is instantly recognizable.

Behaviour Barn Owls favour open countryside, hunting along field edges, scrubby areas, dykes, ditches and woodland borders. During the winter months and the breeding season, they can often be seen in daylight hours. They feed mainly on rodents, and nest in barns, special owl boxes and hollow trees. Adults need good weather, sympathetic landowners and a large supply of mammals to succeed in fledging their young.

Call A piercing, eerie shriek, often given in flight.

The distinctive *alba* race has rich yellow-buff upperparts, mixed with greys, blacks and browns. The short tail shows three grey bars, and the underparts are white.

▲ Dinner is served: adult birds work extremely hard to keep their offspring nourished. Note the broad, rounded wings.

▶ The young soon lose their down (bar a few tufts on the head) as the familiar plumage begins to moult through.

Occasional visitors to Britain, the *guttata* race
of owl is considerably darker on the upperparts,
with rich buffy-brown underparts and a greyish-
brown wash to the heart-shaped face.

Little Owl

21–23 cm (8$^1/_2$–9 in)

Appearance A distinctive, boldly spotted bird, the Little Owl is small, squat and broad-headed, with a short tail.

Behaviour Introduced to Britain in the late nineteenth century, Little Owls soon spread to colonize most of England and Wales. Favoured habitats include parkland, farmland and gardens in rural, suburban or urban areas. They can be encountered at almost any time, as they are generally more active during the day than other owls, and are often seen perching in full view on chimney pots, telegraph poles and posts.

Call A feline *kee-uw*. During the breeding season, a variety of canine-like yelps or even barks may be heard.

The broad, dusky white supercilium extends round to the back of the nape, and is joined by another white stripe from below the bill, creating a 'mask'-like effect.

The fierce, bright yellow eyes are particularly striking, while the white stripes around the head give the bird an almost grumpy look.

◄ Little Owls have a fast undulating flight, and are capable of easy movement on the ground when searching for food. Note the rounded wings.

► As the sun sets, Little Owls become very active, and can often be heard calling from their perching positions.

◄ Juveniles have more downy-looking plumage, and the underparts appear more streaked than spotted. The face pattern is very subdued.

Tawny Owl

36–40 cm (14–15½ in)

Appearance A large-headed and decidedly stocky bird, despite its reasonably long body, the Tawny Owl has complex, intricate plumage in either red or grey tones.

Behaviour These nocturnal owls are found in cities, towns and open countryside, in woodlands, parkland and gardens. More likely to be heard and not seen, if encountered at all it will be at the very depths of dusk, or perhaps caught in headlights perched on roadside signs or posts.

Call The Tawny Owl is responsible for *the* owl call, although the hooting is closer to a long, drawn-out *oo-ooo-hooo* rather than the fabled 'too-wit, too-woo'. Listen also for the pentrating *kee-wick* call.

The 'red' phase is the most
common form in Britain. Note the
two white mirrored 'C' shapes
near the bill, and white lines
extending to the hindneck.
The warm brown upperparts
show all manner of dark
streaks, bars and fringes.

▶ In flight, the Tawny Owl appears round-winged, square-tailed, dark above and pale below. Check for the barred tail and underwing.

◀ The 'grey' form is rarely seen in Britain. The plumage patterns are identical to the more familiar 'red' birds, except that the rich rufous-brown colouration is replaced by cold ashy-grey tones.

Juvenile Tawny Owls have a very striking inquisitive look about them, as their large black eyes peer out from a mass of down and feathers.

Kingfisher

15–16 cm (6–6½ in)

Appearance Instantly recognizable, the colourful Kingfisher has a large head, thick-based dagger-like bill, short wings and a short tail.

Behaviour Kingfishers favour secluded waterways, but can be seen on almost any river, stream, fishing lake, gravel pit or garden pond. They can be notoriously difficult to see, despite their spectacular colour scheme, and spend a great deal of time sitting on half-hidden branches over quiet rivers, waiting for a chance to prove their prowess. At other times, they can be noisy beasts, squabbling over territory or planning intimate liaisons.

Call A piercing, piping *chee*, which can be heard several hundred metres away.

◄ Kingfishers speed past as they fly by, a whoosh of colour. If you're lucky, you may catch a glimpse of the white neck patch and orange cheeks and underparts.

► The brilliant turquoisey-blue upperparts contrast with the greener-looking flight feathers. If nervous, Kingfishers bob their heads and flick their tails before whirring off at great speed.

▶ In search of a fish dish,
the Kingfisher plunges into
the water, wings held back,
neck extended, bill thrusting
forward, and then SPLASH!

▼ Though still snazzy, juveniles
have more subdued colouring
and rougher head plumage
than adults.

▼ Adept fishermen, they secure their prey by grasping it between their mandibles. They will hover before diving if no perch is available.

▲ Kingfishers nest along 'softish' river banks, to ensure they have an easy dig as they excavate the nest tunnel. They will lay five to seven eggs, and usually have two broods in a season.

Green Woodpecker

30–33 cm (12–13 in)

Appearance A long, robust-looking bird with a distinctive crimson crown, the Green Woodpecker has a powerful, sharp bill, large feet (with two toes forward, two toes back) and a short, spiky tail.

Behaviour They can be found in almost any wooded area, from cities to the open countryside. Although primarily a tree-loving species, they are very much at home on the ground, and can be seen hopping about on short-turf areas in search of insects, when not flying from tree to tree in their characteristic undulating manner.

Call A far-carrying, ringing 'laugh' or *yaffle*, often heard when they are treeward-bound, but also when perched.

◀ Females can be identified by a wholly black moustache. On males, the moustache shows a red centre.

▶ The stiff tail acts as a support. Note the grey and white notches on the outer wing feathers.

▲ Seen in flight, the yellow rump contrasts clearly with the comparatively dark olivey-green wings and tail.

▼ Deep beats are followed by closed wings as the bird progresses rapidly from site to site, with a final huge upward sweep to the nearest trunk.

▼ Often seen probing the ground for food (usually ants), Green Woodpeckers feed using their long, sticky tongue.

Juveniles show fine black streaking on the head, and lack the familiar moustache, while the underparts are pale with marked streaking and barring.

Great Spotted Woodpecker

22–24 cm (8$\frac{1}{2}$–9$\frac{1}{2}$ in)

Appearance This medium-sized pied bird, easily identified by its head and undertail plumage, shares the same characteristics as the Green Woodpecker: thick pointed bill, graduated tail and 'reverse' toes.

Behaviour An ever more common garden visitor, particularly in the winter, this woodpecker will take full advantage of rind, suet and nuts left out for it. Away from gardens, they can be found in most woods and copses in any suitable area – villages, cities or open spaces.

Call An explosive, excited *chick*, mainly given in flight. In spring, a loud 'drumming' noise, made by tapping on a tree at a rapid rate (faster than any other woodpecker), often betrays their presence.

▲ Females lack the striking red patch on the rear crown. Other plumage patterns match the male, including the brilliant-red undertail coverts.

▶ The outer tail feathers are white with black notches. Note the longer central tail feathers.

The bold white shoulder patches and white spotting on the wings really stand out during flight, while the red vent clearly contrasts with the black and white graduated tail. The flight action is particularly undulating.

Juveniles show an entirely red crown, while the black moustache is thinner and often streaked white. The underparts are not as snowy white, and the red on the vent is decidedly duller.

Lesser Spotted Woodpecker

14–15 cm (5½–6 in)

Appearance Smallest of the European woodpeckers, this round pied bird has a distinctive barred back, small sharp bill, and the familiar woodpecker combination of graduated tail and 'reverse' toes.

Behaviour These shy birds favour parks and woods, even in cities, and are easiest to see in late winter and very early spring, when leaves have yet to emerge and the woodpeckers become quite vocal. They will rarely – if ever – be seen on the ground.

Call A piercing, almost Kestrel-like *kee kee kee*, often-heard in early spring, and also a rarely heard, quiet *kick* call note. The 'drum' is longer and more constant, but less powerful, than that of the Great Spotted Woodpecker.

▶ Females can be identified by their whitish crown, compared to the neat red crown of the male.

◀ The broad black moustache extends slightly onto the cheek before curving up onto the side of the throat. Note the striking barring on the back. There is no red on the underparts.

▶ The typically undulating flight is a little slower than that of other woodpeckers. From above, the barring across the back and wings is clear.

◀ Due to their size, the 'Lesser Spot' is able to feed on smaller branches and twigs than the bulkier woodpeckers.

Juveniles superficially resemble
adults, except for a whitish forehead,
sometimes flecked black, spottier
flanks and a buffy wash to the face.

Swift

16–17 cm (6½ in)

Appearance This dark torpedo of a bird is instantly recognizable, thanks to its scythe-shaped wings and short forked tail.

Behaviour Summer visitors from Africa, Swifts can be seen anywhere, whatever the area – city, town or hamlet – from late April to August or early September. As long as it has eaves to nest under, the Swift is happy. If the weather suddenly turns bad, Swifts move away to more hospitable areas, before returning after the storms have subsided. Adept and competent fliers, these aerial feeders can display a variety of shapes when airborne.

Call A shrill screaming, often heard in chorus as the flocks fly low over rooftops on summer evenings.

▶ The plumage is almost wholly dark brown, except for a small whitish throat patch. Note the tiny black bill, and subtle contrast in wing colour.

▶ When soaring, the wings are held forward and the tail is open. In fast flight, the tail is closed, and the wings are kept back, with very quick beats.

▶ As the parties of screaming Swifts career over rooftops, they seem to delight in their unrivalled skill in the air, almost shrieking their pleasure to let everyone know just how good they are.

◀ When Swifts make 'landfall' they are immediately transformed from majestic flying machines to ungainly, sad-looking birds, grimly holding onto the surface as if their life depended on it.

Juvenile Swifts are hard to separate from adults when seen on the wing. At close range, however, they appear browner and more scaly, with white flecks on the forehead and a more extensive white bib on the throat.

Swallow

16–22 cm (6½–8½ in)

Appearance Swallows are slender birds, distinguishable from Swifts and House Martins by their size, pointed wings and deeply forked tail with elongated streamers.

Behaviour This herald of spring arrives from Africa in early April, leaving in October. As with other aerial feeders, they can be encountered in any situation, from coastal marshes to urban streets. When not flying to and from their mud nests on the sides of houses and outbuildings, they sit on telegraph wires, chattering cheerfully, before floating off to feed, either singly or in small groups.

Call A tinkling and merry *vit vit* or an occasional *spleeplink*. Their song is a strong, clear, rather fast and prolonged twittering warble.

▶ Swallows have a small, rounded, deep glossy blue head and a chestnut face. The blue extends to the rump, shoulders and upper breast, forming a neat band.

▶ The males have longer tail streamers, although this feature becomes obsolete as the season progresses and the tail feathers wear away.

▶ In the autumn, Swallows congregate on telegraph wires and TV aerials, in preparation for their journey south of the Sahara. Hundreds stop off to feed at coastal reedbeds and roost among the reeds.

▲ In flight, the deeply forked tail gives the Swallow a graceful air. Note the white forewing, pale belly and white spots on the underside of the tail.

Juvenile Swallows have duller
upperparts, and the face is
more dirty orange than chestnut.
The breast band appears
quite smudged, and the
tail streamers are
very short.

House Martin

12–13 cm (4½–5 in)

Appearance Smaller and more compact than the Swallow, House Martins can be easily identified by their white rump and shorter, more moderately forked tail.

Behaviour This familiar summer visitor stays from April to October, and can be found anywhere, making ample use of human habitation for nesting sites. House Martins spend a good deal of time in the air, but, unlike Swifts and Swallows, can also be seen on the ground, collecting wet mud for use as nesting material. In fine weather, they frequently hunt for insects high in the air.

Call A short hard *chirrup*, often heard as they fly by at lower levels, and a distinct *tseep* alarm note. Their song is a soft twittering.

▼ From below, the white body contrasts against the wholly dark underwings and tail, and the head appears capped.

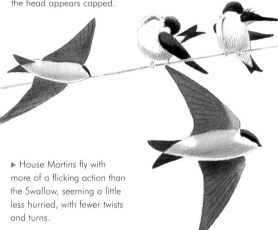

▶ House Martins fly with more of a flicking action than the Swallow, seeming a little less hurried, with fewer twists and turns.

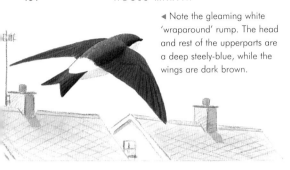

◀ Note the gleaming white 'wraparound' rump. The head and rest of the upperparts are a deep steely-blue, while the wings are dark brown.

◀ Favourite of all nest sites is the 'under the eaves' position. House Martins will return to the same building year after year.

◀ The juvenile (*left*) is a dull version of the adult (*right*), with a dingy wash to the underparts, and browner wings with white tips to the tertials and primaries.

▶ Their bare parts can be seen well when they make touchdown to collect mud. Note the white-feathered legs.

Grey Wagtail

18–20 cm (7–8 in)

Appearance The slim lines, very lengthy tail and overall plumage markings distinguish the Grey Wagtail from the Yellow Wagtail, and make it an easy bird to identify.

Behaviour During the breeding season, Grey Wagtails are found only alongside running water, but in the period outside the nesting season they can be seen around lakes and ponds, and even city-centre rooftops. They are very active birds, constantly on the move, as they dip from rock to rock in search of food, their long tail always wagging.

Call A ringing, metallic *st-it* or *tzit* note, uttered both in flight and at rest.

▶ Females lack the black throat patch, and have less yellow on the breast. Note the black tail with white outer feathers on both sexes, and closed black wing with white edging.

◀ In his summer outfit, the male is a very handsome bird.

▶ In flight, the long black and white tail and yellow rump are obvious. Look on the upperwing for the white bar dividing the grey of the forewing and the black of the hindwing, and listen out for the distinctive call note.

▶ Juveniles look like females, though have buffier upperparts, and faint white wing bars may be apparent. The rump and undertail will be greener than on the adults.

▶ In the winter months, the male Grey
Wagtail loses his black throat and his yellow
breast becomes very pale, while the
yellow on the female becomes
more buffy-white.

Pied Wagtail

17–18 cm (6¹⁄₂–7 in)

Appearance No other bird shows these distinctive plumage characters coupled with a thin bill, rounded body and long wagging tail.

Behaviour Found in any location, from city gardens to coastal marshes, Pied Wagtails are very approachable, having little fear of people, and feed and breed quite happily in close proximity to human activity. These busy birds provide hours of pleasure, darting, flicking, running and chasing off in search of insects. Large flocks are a familiar sight around city streets during the winter, as they fly to roost among trees at dusk.

Call A high-pitched *chiz-zik* or *seel-vit*, often called during flight. The song is a simple warbling twitter.

In the summer, the sexes are similar. Both show a large black bib and black wings with white edgings to the main feather groups. The female (*below*) has a greyer back and less black on the head and breast.

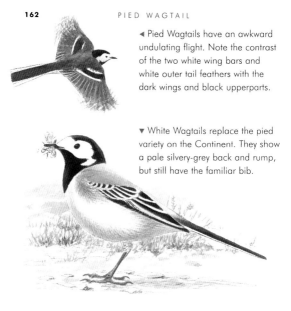

◄ Pied Wagtails have an awkward undulating flight. Note the contrast of the two white wing bars and white outer tail feathers with the dark wings and black upperparts.

▼ White Wagtails replace the pied variety on the Continent. They show a pale silvery-grey back and rump, but still have the familiar bib.

▼ Juvenile Pied Wagtails are a grey and brown version of the adult, with a white 'ear-covert frame', buff-white throat, and nondescript greyish bib.

▼ The first-winter male looks almost identical to the adult female: look for a browner tint to the back and a dark grey (not black) crown.

Waxwing

17–18 cm (6½–7 in)

Appearance This portly bird, with its distinctive head crest and eye stripe, conspicuous yellow-tipped tail and waxy-looking red tips to the upper flight feathers (hence the name), is truly unique – and unmistakable.

Behaviour These autumn and winter visitors do not breed in Britain, but every few years or so irrupt in large numbers, prompting erratic invasions. They may be encountered in gardens, parks or country lanes – anywhere with suitable berry-bearing shrubs and trees, on which they will feed voraciously.

Call A delightfully gentle, whistling *sirrr*, which is very easy on the ear.

▼ The male shows a jet-black eye mask and bib, and marked waxy red tips. Note the white and yellow 'v' tips on the wing.

▲ Females have a smaller crest and sootier bib, and less obvious waxy red tips and yellow tail band.

Waxwing flocks move very quickly, and despite their dumpy appearance they are very adept fliers. The shape in flight is reminiscent of Starlings, although Waxwings look thinner. From below, the black bib, cinnamon breast, rufous vent and grey/yellow tail are clear. From above, note the russet crown and black and yellow tail tip.

Juveniles lack some of the adults' panache, with shorter crests and browner plumage. The waxy red tips are usually missing and the yellow on the tail is not very bright.

Wren

9–10 cm (3½–4 in)

Appearance This tiny, round bird has a short cocked tail, rich brown plumage and pointed, slightly decurved bill, and – even in silhouette – is instantly recognizable.

Behaviour One of the commonest garden birds, Wrens are full of energy, always actively seeking food or shelter. Outside the garden, they are particularly abundant in woodland, and also often found around scrubby areas, farmland and reedbeds. Secretive by nature, they can be hard to spot as they seek food in the cover of tangled undergrowth. Be patient, however, and they will soon reveal themselves on top of a bush or a garden fence.

Song Explosively loud, high-pitched and trilling. Also a rapid-fire scatter-gun scold: *cherr, cherr, cherr*.

◄ Familiar sight: perched on a bramble, the Wren delivers its explosive scold with bill opened to reveal glowing yellowy gape.

► The Wren is delicately marked and full of tone. Look for the fine barring on the upperparts, flanks and wings, and rich rufous hue of the rump and tail.

▶ Flurry of activity: Wrens whirr their short, rounded wings furiously — too fast to see the flaps — as they hurry from cover to cover.

▼ During the depths of winter, Wrens utilize nestboxes as a communal roost site. A peek inside could reveal up to thirty birds tightly packed together for warmth.

Wrens build perfectly
round nests, usually of dead
grass and vegetation, and lined
with moss or discarded feathers,
often among brambles to lessen
the chance of predators.

Dunnock

14–15 cm (5½–6 in)

Appearance Superficially resembling a sparrow (hence the still popular name Hedge Sparrow), the Dunnock is less dumpy, with a thin bill, longish-looking tail and distinctive (if not a little drab) plumage.

Behaviour This shy and retiring bird favours dense and scrubby habitats, from coastal gorse bushes to woodland bramble clumps, or simple garden hedges. They are often seen darting in and out of cover, creeping furtively over lawns. A rather endearing species, they have a lovely intimate courtship display and sweet warbling song.

Song A high-pitched, clear and very resonant *sissisisis*. The strong call note *seeh* is usually heard well before they appear.

This rather dark bird's boldly streaked mantle, wings and flanks offer some contrast with the dull grey head and breast. The vent and undertail are a buffy off-white.

▶ If you see a perched Dunnock, you may be able to spot faint white flecking on the brown ear-coverts and a faint white wing bar, at close view.

◀ During late winter and early spring, the male enters into a delightful display to woo a mate. When near to a likely looking female, he flicks one wing then the other in turn for several minutes. This usually solitary bird may end up attracting a crowd of like-minded wing-flickers!

Duller than adults, juveniles lack the strong rufous tones, and the underparts show heavy black blotches on the breast extending to the flanks, with a whiter throat and undertail.

Robin

13–15 cm (5–6 in)

Appearance The plump, rotund shape and familiar red breast of this most popular of garden birds make it instantly recognizable.

Behaviour Robins are found in a variety of woodlands, parks and gardens, and can be quite tame. In the autumn and winter, the population swells as Continental birds move across the North Sea, sometimes in large numbers. Robins have a variety of familiar postures – strutting, inquisitive, but always on the move. Males require little prompting to burst into song, and cold winter days are often enlivened by this red-breasted serenader!

Song A delightful warbling, heard all year round except during late-summer moulting. Also a *tic tic tic* alarm call.

◀ Garden highlight: Robins love to pick an obvious perch from which to sing, and they will dominate the dawn chorus!

▶ There's no mistaking the bold orangey-red face and breast on these small, fat birds.

◄ Prone to short flights, often close to the ground, Robins move from perch to perch with little flicky flights, darting onto the ground as they go.

► Quick hops are punctuated by short stops, when the wings droop, the tail cocks and the head is held slightly to one side … and then it's off again!

The head, upperparts and breast of the juvenile are liberally speckled with dark brown spotting and scalloping, and a bold white eyering is easily seen. Juveniles moult into their red-breasted garb between June and September.

Fieldfare

24–27 cm (9½–10½ in)

Appearance Reminiscent of the Mistle Thrush in size and shape, this large, round-looking thrush has distinctive chestnut, grey, yellow, white and black plumage.

Behaviour Mainly winter visitors, Fieldfares do breed in small numbers in Scotland and northern England. They like to nest along woodland edges, but on the wintering grounds can be seen in almost any habitat, especially open arable fields, hedgerows and gardens. They commonly associate with other thrushes, particularly Redwings, forming large roving flocks which can quickly devour a berry-filled hedge. In harsh winter weather they will seek food in gardens, and are fond of windfall apples.

Song A harsh, loud, chattering *chak, chak, chak*.

Note the black arrowheads extending from the chin to the rear flanks, and yellowy wash to the breast. The female (*left*) is a little duller, and shows fewer arrowheads.

▶ Often seen in large loose flocks, the wayward and erratic flight pattern is a useful field point. Close up, the white on the underwing can be clearly seen.

▶ Characteristic view: a Fieldfare perches with wings held drooped and tail slightly cocked. Note the contrast between the russet-coloured mantle, grey rump and head and blackish tail.

▼ Juvenile or first-winter birds are duller than adults. The back is brown, with dark feather centres and indistinct white edges, while the underparts show a dingy buff wash and the black markings are less clearly defined.

Blackbird
24–27 cm (9½–10½ in)

Appearance Showing all the classic thrush traits, Blackbirds are quite stocky, with a plump body, rounded head, longish wings and longer tail.

Behaviour Blackbirds are one of the commonest garden birds, and frequent a broad range of habitats in every possible garden context. The resident population is augmented in autumn and winter, with the arrival of birds from the Continent. Blackbirds hop, run and flick their wings and tail in various degrees of agitation, and will also scurry under cover at the merest sign of danger.

Song Full of flutey notes and delivered with breathtaking clarity. They are one of the garden's champion songsters. Also a *tchook* call when agitated.

The male (*below*) is the only jet-black garden bird in Britain, and the bright orange-yellow eyering and bill make it unmistakable. Females (*right*) vary from rufous to olivey grey-brown, and the pale throat shows dark streaks.

▶ Resident males make their
intentions very clear from early
January onwards, delivering
their delightful song from any
suitable perch, be it a rooftop,
TV aerial, wall or treetop.

◀ Signs of adulthood:
a first-winter male shows
dull black upperparts
and dark brown wings,
with a dark bill and
yellow eyering.

▶ Pictured in a characteristic tail-cocked pose, juvenile Blackbirds appear more rufous than the adult female, and are more heavily mottled on upper- and underparts.

◀ Albinism (partial or total) is relatively commonplace, with birds showing random white patches. Sometimes males exhibit a white breast gorget, and may be confused with a Ring Ouzel (*left*); albinos tend to show other white markings.

Song Thrush

22–24 cm (8$\frac{1}{2}$–9$\frac{1}{2}$ in)

Appearance Not to be confused with it spottier cousin the Mistle Thrush, the Song Thrush is smaller and more compact, and lacks the pale wing fringes. Look also for the shorter tail and less boldy marked breast.

Behaviour Song Thrushes are regular visitors to gardens of almost any size, parks, hedges and woodland, and are often seen around human habitation. Further north, they favour damper plantations and forests. In autumn, the population is swollen by Continental migrants streaming into the country from September to November.

Song A clear, languid, flutey affair consisting of much mimicry and repeated phrases. Also a thin *tsip* call in flight, and a loud *chuck chuck* alarm call.

▶ Song Thrushes can often be seen dashing snails against an 'anvil', such as a stone or tree root, to break open their shells (especially in winter, when hard ground prevents access to a ready supply of worms).

◀ Note the finely spotted cheek patch and indistinct buffy supercilium. The bold black spotting extends from throat to rear flanks.

▶ Once one phrase has been sung three or four times, a new phrase will take over. Often delivered from a high perch, the song can be heard at almost any time of year on a fine day.

◀ Note the orangey colour on the underwing – the only common thrush to show this pattern. The flight itself is quick and very direct.

The juvenile is similar to the adult bird, but shows paler marks on the mantle, a more buffy wash to the underparts and smaller spots on the underside. Like the adult it has a black eye, complete with obvious orbital ring.

Redwing

20–22 cm (8–8½ in)

Appearance Superficially resembling the Song Thrush, Redwings are smaller and darker, with a distinctive face and underpart pattern, stubby bill and red underwing.

Behaviour Chiefly autumn and winter visitors, they do breed in Scotland in small numbers, in birch forests or bushes, old tree stumps and even hedgerow banks. On the wintering grounds, they behave in much the same way as the Fieldfare, feeding in berried trees, open fields and woodlands. In hard winters, they feed in gardens with other thrushes – windfall apples are a favourite.

Call If disturbed, they will fly off with a thin, high-pitched *tzipp*. Also a variable, weak song, consisting of short repetitions of three or four flutey notes.

▶ Look for the bold whitish supercilium and moustache, which extends towards the cheeks.

◀ The wing shows darker feather centres, while the white underparts show slender streaks from bill base to flanks.

◀ The most obvious feature in flight is the red on the flank and the underwing. Flocks tend to be disorderly.

▼ A very gregarious bird, the Redwing feeds in flocks, and the birds often bound and hop along the ground in synchrony.

A first-winter bird is almost identical to an adult, except for white or buffy tips to the greater coverts on the wings. From behind, they appear a cold ashy-brown, with the exception of the stripy head pattern and clearly fringed wing markings.

Mistle Thrush

26–28 cm (10–11 in)

Appearance Larger than a Song Thrush, the Mistle Thrush has an elongated, long-tailed shape, more rounded spots on the breast and white underwings.

Behaviour A little more secretive than other thrushes, they can be found in gardens, coniferous woods and parkland, as well as farmland. Their numbers can rise with the arrival of Continental birds during the autumn and winter months. Though they take worms, spiders and insects, they mainly feed on fruit and berries. And they don't eat mistletoe, despite their name!

Song Similar to that of the Blackbird, but tends to be more raucous, quicker, and a little lacking in melody. Also a 'football rattle' call, uttered in flight.

◀ Adults stand more erect than other thrushes, and can look quite 'pigeon-chested', particularly when the wings and tail are held drooped.

▶ Note the yellow wash on the flanks, and white undertail-coverts with few, if any, marks.

▲ The large size and undulating flight are instant giveaways. Look for the white underwings and white tips to the outer tail feathers.

▶ Male Mistle Thrushes always head to the top of a tree to sing. They begin singing in late February or early March, and the breeding season will last into June.

Youngsters appear quite spotted and streaked on the whole of the upperparts. The face pattern appears plainer, but the wings are well marked – even more so than those of the adults.

Garden Warbler

13–15 cm (5–6 in)

Appearance The Garden Warbler is a small, plump bird with a decidedly round head, short tail and stubby bill. Its large eyes and plain face give it a gentle expression.

Behaviour These common summer visitors from Africa are skulking, shy birds, and can be difficult to see, favouring scrubby areas, particularly along woodland fringes or in dense hedgerows or undergrowth. Closely related to the Blackcap, they have similar habitat preferences, although Blackcaps arrive earlier in the spring, and will chase Garden Warblers out of their territory. Both enjoy feeding on blackberries before migrating for the autumn.

Song A pleasing, soft song very like the Blackcap's, but a little quicker and longer. Also a harsh *tac-tac* call.

A close view reveals subtle tones to the seemingly nondescript olivey-brown plumage, with a paler rump, darker flight feathers and tail, and diffuse grey tinge on the side of the neck.

Often the harsh
'tac-tac' call can be
the first clue to a Garden
Warbler's whereabouts, when they are
hidden in deep cover. The male will then
work his way out towards the top of the
bush and begin to sing.

Juveniles have 'fresher-looking' plumage, being browner on the upperparts and washed a stronger buff on the underparts. The bare parts are as those of the adult.

Blackcap

13–15 cm (5–6 in)

Appearance Of a similar build to the Garden Warbler, but with a slightly longer body and slimmer lines, the Blackcap's sharply defined cap (in both sexes) makes it instantly recognizable.

Behaviour Blackcaps are generally summer migrants breeding across the whole of Europe, but are now also increasingly common winter visitors, particularly in milder areas. Hard to track down and locate once trees come into leaf, Blackcaps like to keep hidden, though they are less retiring than Garden Warblers.

Song A melodious, rich combination of warbles and mimicry, more distinct than the Garden Warbler's, with shorter phrases. Also a scolding *tac-tac*.

▶ Females have a rich russet-brown cap, with a browner wash to their plumage. Note the white lower eye-crescent in both sexes.

▲ The male's glossy jet-black cap contrasts with the silvery cheeks and nape and silvery-grey upperparts.

Blackcaps are not renowned for singing from the treetops, preferring to advertise themselves from the cover of a hedge or other tallish vegetation.

Young males can be identified
by softer-coloured underparts,
brownish-washed upperparts and
a dark cap which shows mixed
black and brown feathers.

Chiffchaff

10–11 cm (4–4$^{1}/_{2}$ in)

Appearance Almost identical to the Willow Warbler, the Chiffchaff is *slightly* smaller, with a more rounded head, shorter wings and a stockier appearance.

Behaviour Common across much of Europe in the summer, Chiffchaffs can now also be found as winter residents. During the autumn, the population is bolstered by generally greyer-looking birds from Scandinavia and even Siberia. In the breeding season, Chiffchaffs are seen in almost any type of woodland; during winter, they are frequent visitors to gardens in urban or rural settings.

Song A monotonous, repeated *chiff-chaff* (hence the name), heard from March to June, and less so in autumn. The contact call is a plaintive *hueet*.

The head and upperparts are dull olive-green, while the underparts are buffy-white with a yellowy tinge. Note the pale supercilium, dark eye stripe and pale-looking ear-coverts. Legs and feet are dark, unlike the Willow Warbler's.

Chiffchaffs are alert little birds, often
moving quickly through cover, and
constantly flicking their wings and
jerking from branch to branch.

▶ In the autumn, Chiffchaffs can moult into a brownish or olive guise, fading to brownish-grey with plumage wear.

▶ Young birds are a rich olivey-green on the upperparts and washed yellow below. After their first moult in the autumn, they will soon resemble a grey-washed adult.

Willow Warbler

10–11 cm (4–4½ in)

Appearance Willow Warblers bear a strong resemblance to the stockier Chiffchaff, so check the structural points (the long wing length), the leg colour (pale) and overall plumage tones to help distinguish the two.

Behaviour These summer visitors arrive from Africa in late March/April, departing in September, and are rarely recorded as overwintering. They are found in the same habitats as the Chiffchaff, though tend to favour smaller, younger trees, bushes and ground vegetation, and can also be seen in quiet woodland-fringe or overgrown gardens.

Song A series of fluid descending notes, ending with a rapid flourish. The call note is similar to the Chiffchaff, but a more penetrating and musical *hoo-eet*.

▶ In spring, Willow Warblers are generally paler than Chiffchaffs, with pale olive-green upperparts, a yellow-tinged long supercilium, and cleaner underparts.

◀ Note the thin eye stripe, slightly blotched cheeks, and pale yellow wash to the breast and flanks. The eyering is less obvious than the Chiffchaff's.

◄ Occasionally, pale-looking 'northern' Willow Warblers may be encountered. These striking birds may invite confusion with rarer warblers, so beware!

► An autumn Willow Warbler may look a little browner on the upperparts and more yellowy below.

Some young birds in autumn can be particularly eye-catching, with pale olive-green upperparts and rich lemon underparts, from the face and throat to the undertail-coverts.

Spotted Flycatcher

13–14 cm (5–5½ in)

Appearance Sparrow-sized birds, they show typical flycatcher characteristics of long wings, squarish tail, short legs, big eyes and broad-based bill, and can be identified by their plumage patterns and behavioural traits.

Behaviour These summer visitors are found between May and October. Favourite habitats include suburban gardens, parkland and open woodland. They are often seen darting out from cover in search of food but, when not rushing to and fro, will spend long periods of time on exposed twigs or branches, sitting quietly pumping their tails, before SNAP! – a suitable meal passes by.

Song Rather poor, and made up of several wheezy notes. The call is a thin *tzee*.

◄ Despite their name, adult birds are not spotted at all, but instead show thin dark streaks on the throat, which extend onto the breast.

► The pale grey crown shows dark streaks, which merge into the greyish-brown nape, mantle and rump. Note the white moustache and dark tail.

▶ These agile, acrobatic birds twist and turn in flight – often close to the ground – as they catch assorted flying insects, including bees, butterflies and greenfly, frequently returning to the same perch.

◀ After a late-summer moult, the first-winter bird basically resembles an adult, except for browner upperparts, broader edges to the wing and a prominent bar on the greater coverts.

Juveniles live up to the name, with a heavily scalloped head, mantle and breast, contrasting with the broadly fringed grey-brown wings and dark tail.

Goldcrest

8–9 cm (3–3½ in)

Appearance A tiny, round ball of feathers, this thin-billed bird is plump and compact, with striking markings, and is the smallest bird to be found in Europe.

Behaviour Goldcrests can be seen in many gardens, as well as hedgerows, bushes and woodland, especially coniferous forests. These agile little birds flick constantly from bough to bough, picking at aphids or flycatching, though are equally at home foraging through small bushes and grass. In the winter months, they often join up with the local roving tit flock, as they search for food.

Song The male's song is a distinctive flourishing affair, a *seeh, zeeda-zeeda-sissisyn-see*. The call is a high-pitched, short, rapid *zee zee zee*.

◀ The colour of the crown stripe – bright yellow in females and orangey-yellow in males, bordered black – is the only difference between the sexes.

▶ The pale greyish face contrasts with the olivey green, and gives the large eye a 'surprised' look. The blackish wings show bold creamy wing bars and edges to the feathers.

◄ When displaying, the male raises his crown feathers as a signal to the female. The 'rippling' effect is very striking, as the crown feathers reveal their fiery glory.

▶ These ever-active birds continuously flick their wings during a relentless search for food among trees. They are partial to flies and spiders and also eat beetle larvae, greenfly and moths.

Juveniles are generally duller, with browner-tinged upperparts and no crown markings, except for perhaps some black on the crown sides.

Long-tailed Tit

12–14 cm (4$\frac{1}{2}$–5$\frac{1}{2}$ in)

Appearance The tiny oval body, rounded head, short stubby bill, distinctive plumage and massively long tail make the Long-tailed Tit unmistakable, and always a delight to see.

Behaviour As well as wooded gardens, Long-tailed Tits favour woodland fringe, scrub and dense hedgerows. They are busy birds, always on the move, on a seemingly constant search for food. Family groups gather together in autumn and winter, and the large feeding parties trill their way through gardens and woods, often with other species in tow.

Call The constant contact call, a piercing *tsee, tsee, tsee*, is easily recognizable once learnt.

◄ These highly agile birds often hang upside-down in search of food among the leaves and twigs.

► Note the incredibly small black bill, black eye with red orbital ring, and pink scapulars and flush to the flanks and belly.

◀ Familiar sight: a flock streaming through treetops after the young have fledged.

▶ The small, perfectly round nest is made of lichen, moss, feathers and anything soft, and is built deep inside cover, particularly prickly bushes, or in a tree fork.

▶ In Scandinavia, Long-tailed Tits
have unmarked snowy-white heads
and more white in the wings.

▼ European birds
show broader black
head stripes and
the flanks are a
dingy, dirtier pink.

◀ Juveniles are browner than adults,
with more dark markings on the head
and a shorter tail, and the underparts
show little or no trace of pink.

Marsh Tit

11–12 cm (4½ in)

Appearance This small, compact bird can look surprisingly sleek, despite its thick neck, stubby bill and round head. It is almost identical to the Willow Tit: check plumage markings carefully, and listen for the distinctive call.

Behaviour Marsh Tits can be seen in woods – especially damp broadleaf areas – copses, parks and gardens. They are less inclined to move in large groups, although they do join roving winter flocks, and are more than happy to come to garden bird-feeders. They nest between April and June, producing one brood of six to eight young.

Call The very obvious nasal *pitchou* or *pitchou ke ke ke* is an all-important identifying feature. The song, seldom heard, is a typical tit-like *chip chip* – rapid and ringing.

◄ Note the thick-set neck and smallish head. The plain-looking wings show no wing panel, unlike the Willow Tit's. The brown plumage darkens as it wears in late summer.

► The neat, glossy-looking cap extends to the rear nape, and the white cheeks fade to buffy behind the ear-coverts. The small black bib is a distinguishing feature.

◄ Paler Marsh Tits exhibiting wing panels are found in Scandinavia, adding further confusion with Willow Tits! Pay extra attention to other structural points, and listen out for the voice.

► Even when pristine, the wing markings should be less obvious than on a 'spring-plumaged' Willow Tit.

◄ Marsh Tits use nest holes, but, rather than excavating their own, prefer to make use of natural cavities — even rotten stumps and holes in the ground.

Willow Tit

11–12 cm (4½ in)

Appearance These very close relatives of the Marsh Tit are small, rounded birds with a particularly thick-set appearance, having a large head and 'bullnecked' look. Check structural and plumage characters carefully.

Behaviour Despite their name, Willow Tits are not exclusively 'tied' to willows: favourite habitats include damp areas of woodland, especially alder and birch scrub, as well as conifer areas. They can also be seen in hedges and occasionally at garden feeders.

Call The loud, deep, buzzy *tchay-tchay-tchay* helps distinguish the Willow Tit from the Marsh Tit. The song is a slow, sad *tsui,tsui,tsui*.

▶ The bullnecked look is a distinctive feature of the Willow Tit. Pay close attention to the face and wing markings, noting that pale wing panel.

◀ The black cap is dull, not glossy, and the cheeks are *wholly* white (not white and buff, as on the Marsh Tit). Note also the slightly rounded tail shape (compared to square-ended on Marsh Tit).

◀ The large bib often expands at the lower edge to form a black moustache, always bigger and broader on the Willow Tit.

▶ Willow Tits nest in holes that they excavate themselves in rotten tree stumps, unlike the 'lazy' Marsh Tit, which uses natural holes (or ones already excavated by the Willow Tit!).

► In Scandinavia, Willow Tits are paler, with greyer mantle and wings accentuating the paleness of the wing panel, and the white outer tail feathers are obvious.

◄ As the summer progresses, the pale edgings on the tertials and secondaries wear off, and the distinctive panel is 'lost' – leaving the wing resembling a Marsh Tit's.

Coal Tit

10.5–11.5 cm (4–4^1/$_2$ in)

Appearance Smallest of all the tits found in Britain, this curiously proportioned bird combines large head, small body, short forked tail and thin bill, and its distinctive plumage easily identifies it from other tits.

Behaviour Commonly seen visiting gardens, where they are very partial to nutbags, Coal Tits are found in coniferous woodland in considerable numbers, and also in deciduous woods and hedges. These acrobatic little birds are always moving, appearing restless. They join up with other tits in the winter months, but tend to be a little more solitary, mixing mainly with other Coal Tits.

Song A very distinctive, far-carrying *pitchou pitchou pitchou* or *tisui-tisui-tisui*. The call is usually a thin *tseu*.

▶ Any angle is possible for these agile treetop feeders, although they are also capable ground foragers, probing for insects or rummaging for seeds.

▼ The white cheeks and rear nape patch contrast with the glossy black crown and large bib, and the olive-grey wings show two white wing bars and white tips to the tertials.

Continental birds, particularly those in northern
Europe, have whiter cheeks, a greyer back and
paler buff-pink underparts.

▶ In Ireland, adult Coal Tits show a yellowy wash to the nape and cheeks, and the upperparts are buffier in tone, while the underparts are flushed yellowy-buff.

◀ Juveniles are subdued in colour, with a sooty or brownish bib and crown. The adult's white parts are washed yellow, often strongly.

Blue Tit

11–12 cm (4½ in)

Appearance The Blue Tit's lively disposition, combined with its distinctive plumage colours and head pattern, and almost 'neckless' appearance, make this delightful small bird instantly recognizable.

Behaviour Blue Tits have adapted well to human influence, and are seen everywhere from remote country areas to busy cities. One of the jolliest visitors you will see in your garden, these active birds provide endless entertainment as they search out food or nesting sites. Highly acrobatic, they often hang upside down, their small pointed bill ideal for picking off insects and grubs.

Song A charming, ringing *tsee-tsee-tsirr*. The call is a cheeky, but harsher, *churr-urr-urr*.

The sky-blue crown contrasts with the white and black of the rest of the head, while the yellow underparts (with variable black central streak), lime-green mantle and rump and blue wings (note white bar) make the Blue Tit a ball of colour.

▶ Try attracting Blue Tits to your garden with a nestbox. They may produce two or three large broods in a season, and are always busy ensuring the nestbox stays clean.

◀ Juveniles are yellow, green and black, lacking the trademark blue cap, and are often found sitting in small groups.

◄ Classic view: Blue Tits will peck at milk-bottle tops for several minutes, until BREAKTHROUGH! In goes the head, and the milk is all theirs.

▼ In the autumn and winter, Blue Tits rove with other tits and woodland species. If they struggle to find insects, they are happy to feed on windfall apples and other fruit.

Great Tit

13.5–14.5 cm (5½ in)

Appearance Largest member of the family, the Great Tit is easily identified by its size and distinctive plumage pattern, with bold black central stripe on bright yellow underparts.

Behaviour A real lover of the garden habitat, the Great Tit is one of the most regular visitors to birdtables, feeders, nutbags and bird boxes and, despite its comparatively large size, is still quite an agile feeder. Away from gardens, they can be seen in almost any woodland habitat, parks, hedgerows and even reedbeds.

Song A loud resonant *teecha-teecha-teecha* is the most common song in its repertoire, with other constant call notes including a ringing *zinc, zinc*.

▶ Females are noticeably duller than males, with a narrower central black band on the underparts, sometimes broken or flecked with white or yellow.

◀ Males show a glossy black head and broader stripe on the bright yellow belly. Note the white wing bar and powder-blue rump.

◄ The male starts his characteristic display routine as early as February. With his familiar song he tries to entice a suitable mate, and the pair will, hopefully, raise a brood or two during the breeding season.

▶ After a summer of feeding youngsters and themselves on caterpillars and insects, Great Tits relish the winter months, devouring any nuts, fruit or seeds they can find.

▶ Don't confuse the narrow band of the female (*right*) with that of the juvenile (*below*), as it is distinctly stronger and blacker.

◀ Juveniles appear rather washed-out, with a sooty-brown head and central stripe, a yellowy wash to the cheeks, softer yellow underparts, and dull olive-brown upperparts.

Nuthatch

13.5–14.5 cm (5½ in)

Appearance This sleek, woodpecker-like bird has a compact, torpedo-shaped body, short tail and hefty bill, and shows distinctive markings.

Behaviour Found in parkland and mature deciduous woodlands and gardens, this extremely active bird shows remarkable agility as it climbs along branches and trunks in every possible direction. The Nuthatch is not solely a tree feeder, however, and can often be seen feeding on the ground with distinctive jerky hops. It is also a frequent visitor to garden birdtables and nutbags.

Call When frightened, they will take flight, head for a safe bough and call a loud, full-sounding and excitable *chewit chewit*.

The broad black eye stripe contrasts with the white throat and steely blue-grey upperparts, while the buffy underparts give way to chestnut flanks (paler on the female). Juveniles have brown-tinged upperparts, a narrower, duller mask, and dull flanks.

◄ ► The Nuthatch's undulating flight, along with its size and shape, gives an initial impression of a small woodpecker. Look for the distinctive grey upperparts and orange-buff underparts.

► The sturdy bill is used to great effect when storing or retrieving food. Several hefty blows will break open a stored nut wedged in a bark crevice, and the tapping can be heard for some distance.

▼ Nuthatches are not particularly
shy, and can often be found
foraging through autumn leaf
litter when searching for nuts,
seeds or insects.

Treecreeper

12–13 cm (4½–5 in)

Appearance The Treecreeper is a tiny mouse-like bird with a thin curved bill and a stiff pointed tail, which it uses to 'clamp' onto tree trunks.

Behaviour Found in woodlands, parks and gardens, this shy and unobtrusive bird moves from tree to tree with an undulating flight. Starting at the base of the trunk, it will move stiffly upwards and around, keeping its tail held firmly against the trunk and its feet well spread, picking insects from the bark crevices with its curved bill ... and then the whole procedure begins again.

Call A thin, high-pitched *tsee*, which can be quite tricky to pick up in a bird-filled wood. The song is a succession of accelerating faint high-pitched notes.

Note the white supercilium and distinctive clamped tail shape. The wings show a complex pattern of black, creams, buff-yellow and grey-browns, particularly striking in flight. Treecreepers are often well camouflaged, thanks to their dark brown ground colouring.

▲ In flight, the creamy-yellow wing band and deeply notched tail are clear. Note the contrast between the brown mantle and the paler rump.

▶ The Treecreeper can be elusive in the breeding season. It nests among big clumps of ivy, behind loose bits of bark or in the cracks of trees.

Juveniles are similar to adults, but lack some of the warm brown tones, instead showing a greyish-looking base colour, with fine streaks on the head. The mantle often looks quite spotted and buff, and the rump looks less rufous. Soon after fledging the youngsters will be scurrying around trunks and branches, just like their parents.

Jay
33–36 cm (13–14 in)

Appearance The Jay is the most spectacular member of the crow family to be found in northern Europe, and its chunky build, stout, heavy bill and colourful plumage make it unmistakable.

Behaviour Shy, wary birds, Jays can be found sitting nervously at the edges of woodland, awaiting their chance to drop into a garden for food. They can also be found in local parks and plantations. In exceptional years, Jays from the Continent flood into Britain in the autumn (this irruption is generally attributed to food shortages).

Call With their loud, harsh *kraa*, often fired off at woodland intruders, Jays are more likely to be heard than seen.

The whitish forehead is speckled with fine black streaks, and a fat black moustache contrasts with the gleaming white throat patch. The beautiful aquamarine 'elbow' is notched subtly with black and white.

▶ The flight action is slow and deliberate, but the longer the flight, the more unsteady their course becomes and the more laboured the action appears.

◀ Jays, like other members of the 'corvid' group, can make themselves very unpopular, thanks to their habit of pilfering nests for young or sitting birds, such as defenceless Wrens.

▶ The black, white, pinks and blues of the Jay's upperwing in flight present a brilliant picture. Note the snowy white rump, visible from above and below.

▼ In autumn, Jays congregate in woodlands in small groups to collect and store nuts for the winter, hopping clumsily over the ground in search of acorns.

Magpie

42–50 cm (16½–20 in)

Appearance The black, white and iridescent plumage, chunky, stout black bill and extremely long tail make this familiar bird instantly recognizable.

Behaviour Magpies can be found in a variety of habitats, from hedgerows to coastal bushes, moorland to woodland, and in urban or rural settings. These noisy, chattering birds have a well-founded reputation as a garden-bird terrorist. No garden-nesting species is safe from this pied robber (although this has resulted in other birds learning to conceal their nests more effectively). When on the ground, they hop and sidle along, looking decidedly shifty! The tail is always held up when they walk.

Call A harsh, chattering *chak chak chak*.

Note the delicate blue-green iridescence of the wings and green tail sheen (bluer towards the tip). The white belly and scapular patch contrast with the jet-black head, back, rump and breast.

◀ In winter it is common to see flocks of Magpies leaping through treetops, chattering raucously and always appearing as though they are looking for trouble!

▶ The Magpie's flight action is characterized by quick beats interspersed with glides. The white of the flight feathers and the prominent white 'V' on the back can be clearly seen from above.

▶ Juveniles have a shorter tail, less glossy wings and tail and sooty-looking head and breast, and the white areas are duller. After their first moult in August or September, however, the gloss begins to show.

▼ Baby Magpies can stay calm for long periods, while awaiting the adults' arrival with food. Note the extremely short tail.

Jackdaw

32–34 cm (12$\frac{1}{2}$–13$\frac{1}{2}$ in)

Appearance This compact member of the crow family is distinguishable by its comparatively small size, short bill and distinctive pale grey nape.

Behaviour Found in a wide variety of urban and rural habitats, these highly inquisitive birds have an air of self-confidence as they strut boldly across the ground or over roofs. Adept fliers, they tumble – sometimes en masse – out of the sky, before gliding great distances on suitable air currents. Crow species are renowned for thieving, but Jackdaws in particular have a fondness for stealing shiny objects. Adult Jackdaws, like other crows, mate for life.

Call Jackdaws often announce their presence with a resonant, quite high-pitched *keya* or a harsh *chak*.

The glossy black cap and bib contrast with the pale grey nape, while the sooty-black upperparts show a strong purple-green gloss in certain lights, particularly on the wings. Note the piercing silvery-white eye colour.

▲ In flight, Jackdaws keep their tail closed, but when soaring the tail is fanned and appears rounded. Jackdaw roosts look spectacular.

▶ Urban birds nest in buildings such as churches or in parkland, while rural ones favour trees with suitable nest holes. Jackdaws often breed in loose colonies.

Juvenile Jackdaws show the same plumage patterning as adults, but the colours and tones are duller, and the nape less contrasting.

Rook

44–47 cm (17½–18½ in)

Appearance Bulkier, and less 'tidy-looking', than Carrion Crows, Rooks have a pointed bill, pale face, very high forehead, and shaggy 'trousered' look about the legs.

Behaviour Rooks are found mainly in lowland areas, particularly in agricultural parts, with short-cropped grassy fields being a real favourite. They can also be seen in city parks and gardens. Very sociable birds, they will often join up with Carrion Crows and – in particular – Jackdaws. When on the ground, they appear rather ungainly as they hop and waddle around in search of seeds, insects and worms.

Call Most well known of the Rook's call notes is the distinctive, gentle-sounding *kaah*.

Glossy black with a purple sheen, particularly on the head and wings, Rooks are easily identified by the pale face-patch: the chin, lores and base of the bill show as a large area of whitish bare skin.

▶ Familiar sight: groups of Rooks perch high among the bare trees of winter, congregating around the old nests as nightfall approaches.

◀ When seen closely, the flight shape of the Rook (*left*) is very distinctive. The head looks long, the wings appear pointed and narrower than the Carrion Crow's, and the tail is rounded or wedge-shaped.

◄ In farmland, Rooks can often be seen in fields, searching out various food items, such as worms or root crops and potatoes.

► Youngsters have dark brown plumage and a fully feathered face. They can resemble Carrion Crows: check for size, head shape and those trousers!

Carrion Crow

45–49 cm (17½–19 in)

Appearance These fairly compact-looking birds are neater than the bulkier Rook, and have a heavy black bill, round forehead, flattish crown and square tail.

Behaviour Carrion Crows, and their distinctive (though structurally identical) cousin the Hooded Crow (*see right*), favour open areas of farmland, woodlands, hills, cliffs and moorland, but are equally at home in city parks and gardens. Where the two species of crow overlap, hybrids can often be found. Carrion Crows are particularly opportunistic feeders, with a remarkably well-balanced diet and (as the name suggests) a partiality for all kinds of carrion.

Call A loud, hard *kraa* – the archetypal crow call.

► Hooded Crows, instantly recognizable by their 'pseudo'-pied plumage, replace Carrion Crows in Ireland, northern Scotland and Scandinavia, where the Carrion Crow is generally absent.

▼ Black, with a hint of purple gloss, Carrion Crows may be confused with young Rooks, but note the heftier, rounder bill, 'shorts' rather than 'trousers', and squarer tail.

▶ The square-ended tail and distinctive bulge along the rear edge of the wing, visible in flight, separate this bird from other crow species.

▼ Head and body are held horizontally in this familiar pose, while the trademark 'caw' is delivered – more raucous than the Rook's, and lower-pitched.

Carrion Crows will feed on fruit
and grain as well as insects and
worms, small mammals, birds'
eggs, nestlings and any bit of
carrion they can find.

Starling

20.5–22.5 cm (8–9 in)

Appearance This medium-sized passerine is slightly smaller than a Song Thrush, with a slender pointed bill, peaked head, short tail and quarrelsome manner.

Behaviour The already bulging Starling population swells in the autumn and winter months, with an influx from the Continent. These noisy birds are prolific breeders, making use of any possible hole, whether in a wall, roof or tree – they're not fussy! Their favourite haunts are short-cropped areas of farmland, clifftops and gardens.

Call A grating, harsh *tcheer*. The rather warbly song is a mixture of whistles and clicks, and includes a good deal of mimicry.

A close view reveals a purple iridescent gloss to the head and breast, fading to bottle-green on the flanks. Note the fine flecks (males show fewer spots than females).

In winter, adults change slightly from their glossy summer garb. Both sexes appear quite spotty, females tending to have bolder markings, and the bill changes from yellow to brown.

◄ When they begin moulting to their more adult-like first-winter plumage, youngsters can appear most odd in a 'half and half' transitional mode.

▶ Juveniles appear wholly buffy grey-brown, except for a whitish throat, greyish mottling on the underparts and gingery fringes to the wings.

House Sparrow

14–15.5 cm (5½–6 in)

Appearance Although quite different in plumage, both sexes share a stubby bill (blackish in the male, paler in the female), beady, black eye and pinkish legs and feet.

Behaviour Usually found close to human habitation, the gregarious House Sparrow is the most familiar, and certainly the commonest, of all the birds you will see in your garden, whether in the remote countryside or in the heart of an inner city. Though frequently discarded by birdwatchers as uninspiring and unattractive, unable to do anything but 'cheep' and grub around – albeit cheekily – for crumbs, House Sparrows are, in fact, full of character, accessible to all and show notable field marks.

Call A loud *cheep*, plus various chirps and twitters.

◀ The male's head pattern is distinctive, with a grey crown and nape and black bib. The white cheeks merge into an indistinct half-collar.

▶ Note the creamy patch behind the eye and dark eye stripe of the female, and straw-yellow 'tramlines' on the wings.

◄ Territorial display: squabbles are commonplace and House Sparrows are often seen tumbling in the dust.

► Juveniles bear a close resemblance to the adult female, but are generally brighter, owing to their fresh new feathers. The crown is darker, while the supercilium is a richer honey-buff.

In winter, the male's grey crown is duller
and flecked with white and pale grey, and
the black bib becomes paler, again flecked
white. The upperparts become duller and
the bill changes colour, to yellowish brown.

Tree Sparrow

13.5–14.5 cm (5½ in)

Appearance This handsome bird shows the familiar sparrow shape of big, round head, shortish wings and plump body. Check for the chestnut crown to avoid confusion with the House Sparrow. The sexes are similar.

Behaviour Rural 'cousin' to the House Sparrow, Tree Sparrows are most likely to be found in woodlands, farmland (arable land) and rural gardens, though may also be seen on the edges of villages and towns. Quite brightly coloured, they are a little more inclined to join finch and bunting flocks outside the breeding season than their commoner relative.

Call A resonant, quick *tek tek* can be heard in flight.

◄ The rich chestnut cap and forewing patch, black cheek spot and white collar should all be visible in flight, as may the yellowy pale brown rump.

▼ Note the black eye stripe and cheek patch, smaller bib, two white wing bars and generally warmer tones as further points of identification. The bill shows a yellow base.

Young Tree Sparrows are a more subdued version of the adult, with a greyish wash to the centre of the crown, merging into a duller chestnut cap, and poorly defined cheek spot.

Tree Sparrows nest in loose colonies, either in nestboxes or in excavated tree holes along woodland fringes. Birds nest from April and through to early July, and raise two or three broods.

Chaffinch

14.5–16 cm (5$\frac{1}{2}$–6$\frac{1}{2}$ in)

Appearance The sexes show different colouring, but this stocky-looking finch is distinctive nonetheless: the head shows a noticeable rear peak, the body looks rather pot-bellied, and the tail is slightly forked.

Behaviour This common European bird can be found in deciduous woodland, gardens, parks, farmland, or anywhere bushes or trees are available for nesting. They are great users of birdtables and feeders, hopping around rather awkwardly on the ground. In winter, they become highly gregarious, joining to form substantial flocks – especially with Bramblings – roving in search of food.

Call A soft *chip* in flight, plus a loud *pink* alarm call. The song is short and vigorous, accelerating to a flourish.

▶ The male's slate-blue nape and crown contrasts with a small black patch on the forehead and russet cheeks, while the mantle is a dark reddish-brown.

◀ Lacking the bright colour tones, females show a grey central stripe on the head and grey ear-coverts. The green rump patch is smaller and duller than the male's.

◄ Chaffinches have a bounding and undulating flight. From above, note the double white wing bars, greenish rump and white outer tail feathers.

▼ Though similar to the adult, the immature male (*far right*) shows some grey lines on the head and reddish lines on the mantle.

Autumn and winter males appear a
faded version of their summer selves.
The blue of the head becomes grey
with a hint of brown, and the black
forehead patch is lost.

Brambling

14–15 cm (5½–6 in)

Appearance Although reminiscent of its close cousin the Chaffinch, Bramblings can be identified by several plumage features: less white on the wings and tail, orangey-buff shoulders and breast, and white rump.

Behaviour Mainly winter visitors, Bramblings breed in Scandinavia, eastern Europe and northern Russia, nesting mainly in birch trees or conifers. In winter months, they arrive in western Europe in their thousands, and feed alongside other finches on beechmast, seeds and berries. They can be found on farmland (around grain stores) and in woodland, especially beech.

Call A metallic *tsweek* and, in flight, a rapid *chuc-chuc-chuc*. The song is a repetition of Greenfinch-like calls.

The winter-plumage male (*left*) has a greyish nape to the black head and a black-scalloped mantle, compared to the more drab brown/grey head and brown scalloping of the female.

▶ Although ground feeders, they can be nervous and scare easily, and will fly up into the treetops before cautiously returning to the ground to feed.

▶ From above, the white rump patch is obvious. Other features to look for include the thin off-white wing bars, orange shoulders and forked tail. This winter male shows the distinctive blackish head and back.

◀ In spring and summer, the male has a jet-black head and mantle, with none of the grey tones of a winter bird.

▶ Young birds lack even the greyish wash around the head of most females – brown and black are all they can muster.

Bullfinch

14–15 cm (5½–6 in)

Appearance This 'well-built', round-looking bird has a decidedly neckless look, chunky deep-based bill, rounded wings and a square tail, and is unmistakable thanks to its striking plumage.

Behaviour Bullfinches are resident breeders across most of western Europe (migrating Scandinavian birds may reach north Britain in winter). Favourite habitats include scrubby hedgerows, woodland fringe, orchards, plantations and, especially in winter and spring, gardens. They are seed-eaters, but also take berries and are particularly fond of fruit-tree buds (often destructively so).

Call The flight call is a soft, low, almost whistled *decaw*.

BULLFINCH

The glossy black cap makes a striking contrast with the carmine-red underparts of the male (*right*). The female's underparts are pale fawn with a pink wash, and the mantle is tinged brown.

▲ Both sexes can be easily identified in flight by the black cap, grey or brown mantle, black and white wings, large white rump patch and square black tail.

▶ Juveniles lack the black cap and grey mantle, and are recognizable by their plain, brown head and upperparts and off-white wing bars. The underparts show no red.

▲ Birds of the northern race are larger than British birds, and plumage colouring differs slightly: males are greyer above and lighter red below, while females are also greyer on the upperparts and paler below.

Greenfinch

14–15 cm (5½–6 in)

Appearance This stocky bird has a heavy, stout bill, characteristic of a seed-eater, and short, deeply forked tail. The plumage is variable according to sex, from bright lime-green and yellow to brownish-green and yellow.

Behaviour Greenfinches are especially common in open areas, but can be found in all manner of habitats, including towns and cities, using gardens wherever they can. Like all finches, they are active birds, always on the move (though perhaps not quite as agile as their yellow and green relative, the Siskin), and will flock from autumn through to spring, foraging for seeds and grain.

Song A medley of twittering notes. Calls include a nasal *zwee* and a rapid, trilling *chick, chick, chick*.

The male (*left*) is greener than the female, though both show a yellow edge to the wing and sides of the tail. The female's plumage tends to show streaking.

◄ Impressive display: to attract a mate, a male will deliver his twittering song both from a perched position and also in a delightful, butterfly-like fluttering display flight.

▶ Greenfinches are more inclined to visit gardens in winter. The scenes at feeders can be filled with aggression and squabbling, as birds try to oust each other from their positions.

◄ Shared field marks include the green rump, bright yellow tail flashes, deeply notched black tail fork and yellow blazes on the wing.

▼ Juveniles resemble the adult female, but show more streaking on the upperparts. The underparts are yellowish-grey, and streaked brown.

Goldfinch

11.5–12.5 cm (4½–5 in)

Appearance This small finch is a delicate bird with a largish pointed bill, rounded head, slim body and forked tail, and is instantly recognizable, thanks to its distinctive red, black, white, brown and gold plumage.

Behaviour Goldfinches can be seen in a wide variety of habitats, from scrubby areas of wasteland to clifftop edges, weedy fields, beaches, woodland fringes and gardens. In winter, large flocks can be seen, especially on coasts, roaming between feeding sites. When disturbed, these charming birds present a riot of colour, taking flight with their clear, strong call.

Song Fast, trilling and very twittery. The flight call is a clear, ringing *stickalit*.

The red, black and white head and broad gold wing bar make these delightful birds unmistakable. Males tend to show more red on the face, while females have more grey on the wing.

◀ Note the white rump patch and spots on the tail, visible in flight. The white underparts show tawny 'thumbprints' on the shoulder.

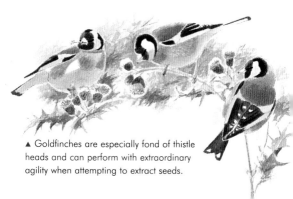

▲ Goldfinches are especially fond of thistle heads and can perform with extraordinary agility when attempting to extract seeds.

Before their moult in the early autumn, juveniles appear very dull compared with adults, with dark streaking on the plumage, but they do show the gold wing bar.

Siskin

11.5–12.5 cm (4¹/₂–5 in)

Appearance This small, rather dumpy finch has a slender, sharply pointed, bill and shortish, deeply forked, tail. Plumage ranges from yellowish- to greyish-green.

Behaviour Favoured habitats include conifer plantations, alder and birch woods and open countryside. In the winter months, they are regular garden visitors, and are particularly attracted to nutbags. These extremely active birds prove to be highly acrobatic when feeding, with flocks moving swiftly from tree to tree in search of food and exploding in a mass from treetops.

Song A simple twittering, delivered from a perch or during a display flight. Distinctive call notes include a wheezy *tsooet* and squeaky *tsy-sing*.

◄ The male has a black crown and bib, contrasting with the green cheeks and yellow face, dark lime-green mantle, and washed-yellow underparts.

► Females are duller, and show more marked streaking. Note the broad, pale lime stripe about the eye, bringing some relief to the head pattern.

◄ Aerial acrobats: a small winter feeding flock displays its amazing agility, a real joy to behold. Flocks maintain a distinctive, constant nasal twitter as they move.

► Juveniles show a distinctive pattern on the breast and flanks, the dark grey smudges contrasting with the otherwise clean whitish underparts. The upperparts are a light grass-green tone, fresher than the adult female's colouring.

◄ Note the long wings, forked tail and yellow tail sides, clearly visibly in flight. The yellow wing bar on the female is a little more subdued than on the male.

► Male rivalry: aggression displays are commonplace. Usually the dispute is merely a show of bravado, but the birds will occasionally tumble off and then recover, only to find another bird has taken their place on the feeder.

Linnet

13–14 cm (5–5½ in)

Appearance Linnets are compact little birds, with a typical finch bill – slender and pointed – and deeply forked tail. Plumage varies from the glorious pink and greys of a spring male to the delicate browns of the female.

Behaviour In the breeding season, Linnets can be encountered in a variety of habitats from coast to heath; at other times they can be seen in stubble fields and meadows, as well as on roadside verges and (though less commonly) in gardens. As with most finches, family parties and winter flocks prove to be highly active, bounding between feeding areas and constantly twittering at each other.

Song A pleasant, musical twitter. Also a *tsweet* call.

A spring male (*below*) is a splendid sight: the rich pink forehead contrasts with the grey of the head, and the breast shows strong pinky-red patches. The streaked brown tones of the female look rather drab in comparison.

◄ In flight, the familiar finch features (forked tail, long wings) are obvious. Note the male's rich russet mantle (*left*), and the white on the shafts of the flight feathers on both sexes.

► Juveniles appear similar to the female, but look significantly brighter. The head, mantle and wings are a richer brown, and the streaking is bolder.

The winter-plumage male is a more subdued version of the rosy-tinted summer bird, with scalloping on the mantle, heavy flank markings and no traces of the bright pinky-red colour.

Lesser Redpoll

11.5–13 cm (4½–5 in)

Appearance As the name suggests, these small, plump finches show a red patch on the forehead (more pronounced on the male). Size and shade of plumage varies between European forms.

Behaviour Common across most of western and northern Europe during various times of the year, Redpolls come in various racial guises, which accounts for their sometimes erratic distribution. Favoured habitats include gardens, parkland and various types of woodland. As with other tree-loving finches, Redpolls are acrobatic and mobile, flocks often whizzing through trees overhead.

Song A buzzing trill. Call note is a rapid and metallic *chuch-uch-uch*.

▶ Females show only a small amount of red on the cap and little, if any, on the breast. The rump tends to be browner, and the flanks are streakier.

◀ Male Lesser Redpolls have a pinky-red wash on the breast, pale pink rump, and more prominent red cap. Note the small black bib in both sexes.

▶ The double buff wing bars and paler rump are visible in flight. Listen out for the buzzing trill as they pass overhead.

▲ Scandinavian Common Redpolls appear larger and paler. The head and upperparts are frosty grey-brown, while the wing bars and rump look whiter.

Redpolls in winter appear browner: both sexes retain the red cap, but the male's pink flush on the breast becomes quite indistinct, and the rump colour becomes duller.

Hawfinch

16–17 cm (6½ in)

Appearance This hulking brute of a finch is unmistakable, thanks to its large head and huge bill, and its distinctive brown, black, grey and white plumage.

Behaviour Hawfinches are extremely shy, wary birds, and very rare garden visitors, favouring deciduous or mixed woodland and parkland. For the best chance to see one, search suitable sites early in the morning, and look out for hornbeams – the Hawfinch's favourite tree. Their powerful bill – steel-blue in the summer, fading to brown in the winter – is easily able to crack open hornbeam seeds, and other hard seeds such as cherry stones.

Call A loud, metallic *zik-zik*, uttered in flight.

The female (*behind*) is generally
duller and more grey-brown than
the male, lacking the rich rufous
tone of the head and bluish-
black flight feathers.

The short square tail and big
head and bill are obvious in flight.
Look for the grey nape and collar,
broad white bar on the inner wing
and tail tip, and white shafts
on the flight feathers.

Juveniles are a grey-brown, scaly version of adults, with a darker mantle, rump and tail, and light scalloping on the plumage.

Yellowhammer

16–17 cm (6½ in)

Appearance This large bunting is an elongated bird with long wings and a longish notched tail, which it flicks constantly. The plumage is distinctive, and even the drab female should be easy to identify.

Behaviour Yellowhammers are found in open country, farmland, hedgerows and – especially in winter – large gardens, where mixed flocks of finches and buntings often become regular visitors, feeding on seed and grain (almost exclusively on the ground). They perch on bushes and telegraph wires to deliver their familiar song.

Song A monotonous series of notes, commonly interpreted as 'a little bit of bread and no cheese'. The call is a sharp *chinz*.

▶ A sight to behold: the male's head glows a sulphurous yellow (particularly in the breeding season), contrasting with the rich olive nape, streaked chestnut mantle and breast patch.

▼ The duller female shows fine streaking on the crown, dark-bordered greyish cheeks and moustache, with a brownish nape and mantle.

First-winter birds resemble adult females, but can be separated: males have a brighter yellow head and underparts, and richer chestnut colouring, while females show a dark-streaked brownish crown and dull olive-yellow head.

▶ Note the tail length – obvious in flight – and look for the deep notch. The streaked mantle, plain chestnut rump, dark tail and white outer tail feathers can all be seen.

◀ Juveniles resemble adult females, but are duller, with more streaks on the head, streaked breast and flanks, and a dull, faintly streaked rufous rump.

Reed Bunting

14–15 cm (5½–6 in)

Appearance Slimmer, less bulky and shorter-tailed than Yellowhammers, Reed Buntings have distinctive breeding and winter plumages, and a small, stubby seed-eating bill, which is convex in shape.

Behaviour This active bird frequents marshes and reedbeds, as well as hedgerows, bushes, farmland (particularly in winter) and, increasingly, gardens. Reed Buntings often associate with other small seed-eating passerines during the autumn and winter, and can be seen feeding in stubble fields, gardens, winter-wheat fields or at special feeding stations.

Song An unforgettable slow wheeze, delivered from an exposed position. Also a loud *tseep* call note.

◀ The spring male's jet-black head and throat contrast with the white moustache and collar. The blackish mantle shows rufous feather edges, with broad yellow tramlines extending to the greyish rump.

▶ Females show different head markings: note the chocolate-brown forehead and crown, streaked with black, and white supercilium and moustache.

▶ Juveniles resemble the adult female, but have a darker head and buffier underparts, with more streaking. Note the brownish supercilium.

◀ Winter females show a greyer head, with a yellow wash on the supercilium and throat, and the breast and flank markings are more pronounced, with longer streaks.

The head pattern of the male Reed Bunting in winter becomes tainted by rufous tips on the feathers, particularly around the lores, supercilium, ear-coverts and throat.

Resources

Useful Addresses

The Wildlife Trusts
The Kiln, Waterside
Mather Road, Newark, NG24 1WT
Tel: 0870 0367711
www.wildlifetrusts.org
www.wildlife-watch.org
*The leading voluntary organization
in Britain, working in all areas of
nature conservation.*

RSPB (Royal Society for the
    Protection of Birds)
The Lodge, Sandy
Bedfordshire, SG19 2DL
Tel: 01767 680551
www.rspb.org.uk
*Britain's leading bird conservation
organization. Offers information,
advice and practical help on attracting
birds. Mail order service available.*

BTO (British Trust for Ornithology)
The National Centre for
    Ornithology
The Nunnery, Thetford
Norfolk, IP24 2PU
Tel: 01842 750050
www.bto.org
*Offers birdwatchers the opportunity
to learn more about birds by taking
part in surveys such as the Garden
BirdWatch or the Nest Record
Scheme.*

CJ WildBird Foods Ltd
The Rea, Upton Magna
Shrewsbury, SYA 4UR
Tel: 0800 731 2820
www.birdfood.co.uk
*Leading supplier of approved birdfood,
feeding equipment, birdtables, and
much more. Online shopping available.*

Further Reading

Attracting Birds to Your Garden,
Stephen Moss and David
Cottridge. New Holland
Publishers, 2000

Bill Oddie's Birding Map. New
Holland Publishers, 2001

Bill Oddie's Birding Pack. New
Holland Publishers, 2001

*Bill Oddie's Birds of Britain and
Ireland*. New Holland Publishers,
1998

*Bill Oddie's Introduction to
Birdwatching*. New Holland
Publishers, 2002

The Bird Table Book, Tony Soper.
David and Charles, 1992

*Chris Packham's Back Garden
Nature Reserve*. New Holland
Publishers, 2001

Cooking for Birds, Mark Golley.
New Holland Publishers, 2006

The Garden Bird Year, Roy Beddard.
New Holland Publishers, 2001

How to Make a Wildlife Garden,
Chris Baines. Francis Lincoln, 2000

Magazines:

BBC Wildlife Magazine
Subscriptions available from: BBC
Wildlife Subscriptions, PO Box 279,
Sittingbourne, Kent, ME9 8DF

Birdwatch
Subscriptions available from:
Warners, West Street, Bourne,
Lincolnshire, PE10 9PH

Birdwatching
Subscriptions available from:
EMAP Active, Bretton Court,
Bretton Centre, Peterborough,
PE3 8DZ

Bird Topography

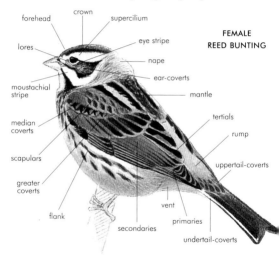

**FEMALE
REED BUNTING**

forehead
crown
supercilium
lores
eye stripe
nape
ear-coverts
moustachial stripe
mantle
median coverts
tertials
rump
scapulars
uppertail-coverts
greater coverts
flank
vent
secondaries
primaries
undertail-coverts